# Four Millennial Plays from Belgium

# Four Millennial Plays from Belgium

Martin E. Segal Theatre Center Publications
New York

Martin E. Segal Theatre Center Publications
Marvin Carlson, Director of Publications
Frank Hentschker, Executive Director
Rebecca Sheahan, Managing Director

# Four Millennial Plays from Belgium

by

Jacques De Decker
Serge Goriely
Jean-Marie Piemme
and
Pascal Vrebos

Edited and Translated by

David Willinger

Martin E. Segal Theatre Center Publications
New York

Library of Congress Cataloging-in-Publication Data

Four millennial plays from Belgium / by Jacques De Decker, Serge Goriely, Jean-Marie Piemme and Pascal Vrebos ; edited and translated by David Willinger.
pages cm
ISBN 978-0-9906847-1-8
1. Belgian drama (French)--21st century--Translations into English. I. Decker, Jacques de. II. Goriely, Serge. III. Piemme, Jean-Marie. IV. Vrebos, Pascal. V. Willinger, David, editor translator.
PQ3846.F68 2014
842'.92--dc23

2014041444



This book is made possible by support from
l'Académie Royale des Sciences, des Lettres, et des Beaux-Arts de Belgique

Cover image © Tang Yau Hoong

Christopher Silsby, Production Editor

Camille Gaume, Publication Assistant


Marvin Carlson, Director of Publications

# Table of Contents

Acknowledgments ix

Introduction xi

*This Is Not a Real Pipe*
by
Pascal Vrebos 1

*The Sorcerers*
by
Serge Goriely 33

*Patriot's Café*
by
Jean-Marie Piemme 81

*The Magnolia*
by
Jacques De Decker 149

About the Authors 218

## ACKNOWLEDGMENTS

The editor wishes to thank the following people, without whom this book would not have been possible: Dr. Peggy Dean and Dr. Kathleen Potts for reading the entire text and making essential suggestions for its improvement. From the Segal Center—Christopher Silsby, Rebecca Sheahan, Camille Gaume, and especially Frank Hentschker for believing in the project and graciously seeing it through to completion. Thanks also to Pinuccia Contino, Claudia Ritter, and all the playwrights whose plays are represented here for their cooperation and good will through the arduous process of translation and publication. And thank you to all my friends in Belgium over the years whose continued hospitality and inspiration keep me coming back.

## INTRODUCTION

Brussels is the capital of Europe. All the regulations governing how farmers may plant crops, how nations manage debt, and how they dispose of waste emanate from Brussels. When President Obama wants to address his opposite numbers in the European Community, he goes to Brussels to do so. When English farmers or Greek taxpayers want to campaign for a divorce from a united Europe, it is "Brussels" that they condemn. As the little ditty on Brussels radio chirps out: "Bruxelles—CAP-I-TALE!" And yet we in the English-speaking world know precious little of the theatre endemic to this nexus of civilization. The present book provides a sampler of some of the best recent plays to come out of an often evoked, but little-understood land—Belgium, specifically the French-speaking part. Three plays are written by playwrights born and bred in the largely French-speaking capital. Only one, Jean-Marie Piemme, was born in Wallonia, but has been widely produced both in the Walloon provinces and Brussels, having become house playwright to one of Brussels' principal theatres, Théâtre Varia.

On the other—the Flemish—side of the language frontier, there has been an extraordinary flourishing of directing talent in the past thirty years—including such bright lights as Gie Cassiers, Arne Sierens, Luk Perceval (now sharing his time between Germany and Flanders), and Ivo van Hove, directing mostly in Holland, whose productions are also frequently on display on this side of the Atlantic at B.A.M., the New York Theatre Workshop, and at Lincoln Center. Many other theatre collectives, such as Needcompany, Compagnie Cecilia, Abattoir Fermé, TG Stan and Ontroerend Goed, further enliven the landscape with constant innovation. The protean theatrical writer Tom Lanoye single-handedly fills up an astonishing degree of the Flemish dramaturgical space, where he churns out adaptations and original works in seemingly inexhaustible fashion as the principal literary collaborator with most of the best directors. Heir to the great Hugo Claus, Lanoye is worthy of several anthologies in English devoted exclusively to his plays, adaptations, and prose.

On the French-speaking side of the linguistic divide, encompassing both Brussels and Wallonia, where theatres also proliferate, there is nowhere near the same level of directorial innovation as in Flanders. For several decades, the Francophone theatre directors have adapted a derivative approach, most often following trends in France, but also those flowing west from Germany. Notably, the Théâtre National de la Belgique typically hosts travelling productions from France rather than cultivating a native repertory company. Of all the traditional performance venues, none has found a signature style or level of accomplishment that distinguishes itself markedly from the theatres of Paris, which they seek to emulate. Whereas the aging segment of the audience on the Flemish side appears receptive to the most far-out experimentation as they freely mix with the hip younger set, that on the French-language side wants the reassurance of old models, the comfort of the familiar. And that's what they get from the obliging directors. It's a chicken or egg situation.

And yet. . . even given this impasse, a number of playwrights have been producing many interesting, even important works. I have here culled four representative plays from Francophone Belgium, written over the last sixteen years—in a collection that can be characterized as "millenial." Today's Belgian playwrights are culturally as cosmopolitan as any in the world, attuned to all the international theatre themes and trends in the air. This tropism toward the international is counterbalanced by distinctly Belgian flavor and tradition, one redolent of harsh comedy and a grotesque vision of the human menagerie. It is exemplified in the visual arts by James Ensor, Felicien Rops, and Marcel Broodthaers, and in the twentieth century theatre of Maurice Maeterlinck, Michel De Ghelderode, Fernand Crommelynck, and Paul Willems, and has been assimilated by varying degrees and diverse methods by three out of four of our playwrights, each of whom makes his own blend of "belgitude" together with contemporary, international sensibility. As we shall see, some of the most challenging of these works don't get produced, because they are—well, *too* challenging.

Pascal Vrebos's *This Is Not a Real Pipe* is a case in point. Vrebos, who is also a television talk-show host and magazine editor—and thus ensconced in the center of the Belgian establishment—has had his plays consistently produced at all the leading theatres of Brussels. And yet this play, arguably his best, has merely had a staged reading in an outlying Brussels neighborhood at the Centre Culturel de Woluwé Saint Lambert. Why? Because it goes too far into a realm of questionable taste. But when one compares it to the works of Sarah Kane, for example, it's quite tame, which is a commentary on what the market will bear in Francophone Belgium.

Written on the subject of Dominique Strauss-Kahn's (generally known by the sobriquet, DSK) famous debacle in a New York hotel room where *something* happened between the all-powerful French statesman and a humble cleaning lady, the play goes straight to the multiple issues which this episode from contemporary history brings up: What really *did* happen? Is a great man immune from social censure, or should he be treated like any other mere mortal in the same position? What does it say about power relationships when the contestants are a vulnerable woman of color and a white man accustomed to wielding unassailable authority at the highest levels of the economic hierarchy? Is there any love or comprehension available for a wealthy predator when caught at an illicit game he may have been getting away with for decades prior? Vrebos sets up a dramatic prism that looks at all these questions from numerous angles by replaying the scene in the hotel in multiple hypothetical ways and by introducing a panoply of interested observers—lawyers, wife, detectives, spies, and friends —to comment on the case and on the offending "JJH" (stand-in for DSK), leaving us with oblique, contradictory points of view to consider. In sharp contrast to the recent film on the same subject, *Welcome to New York*, directed by Abel Ferrara and starring Gerard Depardieu as DSK, *This Is Not a Real Pipe* assumes nothing about what really happened; indeed it appears to show that absolute clarity on what occurred between those two people that day is impossible to obtain. Ferrara's film shoves an open and shut case of sexual abuse into the audience's face, as it tracks an insatiable DSK through revolting orgies, into the holding cells of New York penitentiaries, and then into the luxurious padded cell of a Soho triplex where he and his wife, Anne

Sinclair, holed up during the protracted hearings. The confrontation between DSK and the hotel maid, Nafissatou Diallo, is depicted in that film as a squalid example of forced sex without a drop of ambiguity or nuance. And while it may—who knows?—come close to what actually took place, this treatment is devoid of artistry and depth. One gets the point after the first five minutes: DSK is a self-indulgent goon deserving of severe condemnation. The dialogue appears to be improvised—by actors incapable of improvising skillfully—and the camera-work and editing is determinedly crude and gross—as gross as the story it purports to illustrate.

While Vrebos's play includes the coarseness of DSK's personality and actions, it is but one facet of the narrative, as the author makes space for us to plumb the depths of a complex man, replete with his spoiled upbringing, his propensity for altruistic action on the governmental plane, his ability to relativize all human choice, his fluctuations between self-pardon, self-condemnation, and an understandable desire for the whole mess to just go away. In contrast with Ferrara's, Vrebos's dramatic language is exploratory and multifarious, allowing the characters flights of lyricism even when descanting on the lowest of human drives. While this is the story of a Frenchman and a Caribbean woman, the Belgian play cannot help but evoke Belgium's colonialist past with the Congo, which the European dominating power effectively raped; the Congo eventually liberated itself, but then entered a continued, troubled symbiosis with Belgium. Indeed, Vrebos, with humor and brio, uses a crucial anecdote from current events to open up a plethora of considerations regarding economic, gender, and racial inequality—some of the most important issues of our times. His title, borrowing from the Belgian Magritte's famous image of a pipe ("*pipe*" in French is both a smoking implement and an exact translation of "blow-job"), is intended to challenge our assumptions of what happened in that hotel room, whatever they may be, and by extension, many other complacently held beliefs. And that's not the only thing that is "Belgian" about it. While focusing on an individual who is manifestly French, and setting the play in America, the gustatory humor, the ludicrous but larger-than-life central figure, the generous mix of low farce with bold self-inquiry recognizable from the classical tragic tradition, the special language, an admixture from the sewer and the stars, brand it as a work in the Ghelderode lineage, Ghelderode having been the exemplar of the heady mixture that is identifiably Belgian playwriting in the twentieth century.

Serge Goriely's *The Sorcerers* also foregrounds a relationship between a white European male and an African woman—in this case one within the bounds of a legally sanctioned marriage. Where clichés of Africa might prime us to expect that the transplanted Nigerian woman's family could cast a spell on the white husband who has removed her from their culture, the play posits quite a different situation—one where the husband's white European family, in all open-mindedness, urbanity, and liberality, casts a European-style spell on the African interloper, instigating her descent into madness and ultimate death. In the constellation of the play, the family is determined to wrest the manifestly well-meaning, but hapless husband's loyalties and affections back to their camp and to gain custody over the child who is the fruit of the marriage, first by determining his name (Albert, after the Belgian King Albert I), then by virtually kidnapping his person. Paula, the African woman, is pressured to subjugate her own will to her mother-in-law's domestic authority and allow the older woman's tastes to trump her own in her household, even as her Belgian husband's family and friends defame her character and deride her ability to provide an adequate home environment for her child. The spell is cast both directly and subliminally, but surely unhinges Paula and eventually drives a wedge between her and Luc, the man of the house, who is essentially un-manned through the working of the self-same spell. In Leopold II's Congo, the imperial process was effectuated by cutting off natives' limbs; here the means are more subtle, but no less effective, a stratagem which Strindberg called "psychic murder."

Goriely uses a shifting style—one in which accompanying physical actions are implied, but perhaps abstractly executed, and where the characters speak past and over each other. Normal segments of dialogue alternate with jagged telegraphic blurtings-out. One character speaks, absorbing a second character's answers into their monologue, even though the other character is standing there and able to speak for themselves. Dreams, folk tales and exorcism rituals are interwoven into the phlegmatic ambiance of materialistic, bourgeois Brussels, suggesting a separate inner plane of existence where the real struggle for domination ensues. While Luc's family argues for and uses the parlance of science, medicine, liberal education, and agnostic reasonability, behind it all is unmitigated savagery and blood-lust; Paula struggling to adapt to a new land and culture, under siege by unseen forces whose very existence are always denied, doesn't stand a chance. When she gleans a conspiracy at work against her, she is pooh-poohed as a superstitious backwoods-woman. And thus the conspiracy runs apace, ever gaining strength.

Goriely had trouble getting this play on in a full production. The talkback session following an open, staged reading at Théâtre de la Vie in Brussels found the audience in consensus that the play gave too negative an image of Belgium and was therefore repugnant, good to sweep under the carpet. Perhaps an English-language audience will find otherwise.

Jean-Marie Piemme's *Patriot's Café* takes on an equally unpleasant but topical subject—the resurgence of the Extreme Right. It views the political movement on a personal level, introducing us to typical sorts of common folks from Wallonia—the salt of the earth who are most susceptible to the allure of a right-wing populist siren-song—exposing their love affairs, their yearnings and frustrations, in general putting a human face on a corrosive, but pervasive movement—not to condone it, but helping us understand its allure.

It is ironic that Piemme hones in on this particular milieu, as the Extreme Right in Wallonia in reality has precious little sway compared to so many other hot spots throughout Europe. A strong syndicalist tradition growing out of mining and metallurgy industries have left this half of Belgium firmly in the Socialist camp. That is in sharp contrast with Flanders where neo-Nazism is ever lurking around the edges and where the Flemish Nationalists (as in France, Greece, and Hungary) have been gaining power with every election, most recently becoming the largest single vote-getter in the north of Belgium. But memory of the phenomenon that was Léon Degrelle, the devoted Walloon acolyte to Hitler, can't be altogether dismissed. During World War II this French-speaking Belgian raised and led a committed Walloon Brigade on the Eastern Front, deep into the Soviet Union, championing the Nazi cause. The Extreme Right in recent times gained a maximum of only 7% of the electorate in Wallonia before then splintering and losing parliamentary seats. Their leading proponent was a medical doctor called Daniel Féret, and the character of Leopold Lesca is loosely based on him. Féret proceeded to alienate a large part of his following and got into legal trouble on many fronts—for use of racist language, but also for grand larceny and other non-political crimes. Despite a stint in prison, he has now once again been elected to the Brussels regional parliament, and so is not quite out of the running. Piemme smells potential danger hovering over his native land where high unemployment and xenophobia could breed a rhetoric of hatred and totalitarianism—imagines the form and discourse—at once elitist and proletarian—should the contentious factions of the Extreme Right unite in his back yard behind a convincing, charismatic leader, although it has not managed to do so thus far. Piemme follows in the footsteps of Jean Louvet, another Walloon playwright, who created a poeticized proletarian milieu in such plays as *The Man Who Had the Sun in His Pocket* and *Conversation in Wallonia*, writing of a political landscape peopled with sympathetic, flawed ordinary folk. Here too there is an epic sweep, an attempt at societal portraiture, and a refusal to capitulate to bottom-drawer naturalism. Piemme is striving to find a local post-Brechtian alternative to theatre of the Alienation Effect.

The final play in this collection, *The Magnolia* by Jacques De Decker, in contrast with the others, contains no particularly Belgian aesthetic flavor or social context. It is also the only one that could be considered escapist—if one were to take it on face value and entirely ignore the serious concerns which underlie it. It's a witty situation comedy such as those by English playwrights like Alan Ayckbourn, who, in turn served a spiritual apprenticeship at the knees of Scribe and Sardou. It starts with a premise of a woman who is leading a double life with two boyfriends who don't know of each other's existence. Both imagine they have a monogamous claim to Marie or Antoinette, as the same woman is know to each of them respectively. Marie-Antoinette is attempting to have her cake and eat it too, but the omniscient playwright is too clever to let them go on in ignorance of each other forever. Marie-Antoinette's fine-tuned scheme, which works perfectly for her, only holds together so long as all her unwitting partners act true to type; the minute the boyfriends go outside the boundaries seemingly prescribed by their limited identities, Marie-Antoinette's house of cards comes tumbling down. The boyfriends, from lifestyles seemingly so disparate as to preclude their ever meeting, are brought together through the improbable twin means of garden architecture and water polo, to the detriment of Marie-Antoinette's carefully scaffolded plans. A second complication arises when Marie-Antoinette's lesbian friend, Josephine-Charlotte (the name both of Leopold III's daughter and that of a metro stop in Brussels) decides that she and her partner want to sire children. It is as though there are only five people in the entire world and that they must, perforce, discover each other through a confluence of perverse motives. This extremely clever comedy uses the law of chance which defies all mathematical odds, then transforms into a *lehrstücke* that unmasks the folly of attempting to control odds in your own and everyone else's lives. De Decker's play dramatizes the comeuppance of a woman—a woman who lives anywhere in the western world that boasts both urban and exurban locales—who attempts to realize a life-style outside the norm, dragging unwitting others into the new configuration. Is it an act of feminist empowerment for her to take that volition exclusively into her own hands or one exploitive of her male partners? When both boyfriends break the monogamous bounds with her at a later point, can they be indicted for duplicating the example she has already set? Can monogamy work for anyone at all, or is it in fact simply a hypocritical social convention or trap that only the most gullible fall for?

The social background to this play is neither Belgian, nor even particularly European, but abstract in the way Marivaux's classic French comedies were. In fact, that's what it is: an extremely diverting and witty *marivaudage*. A man of vast influence on the Belgian cultural scene, for many years chief drama critic for Brussels' principal daily newspaper, *Le Soir*, and later its cultural editor, De Decker writes a theatre at variance with the rest of the playwrights in this volume who make no efforts to mask their Belgian identity, two of whom set their plays in recognizably Belgian social and geographical contexts—writing instead a work that could be readily appropriate to a French context, or even a British, Canadian, or American one. He is not the first Belgian to adapt this strategy of delocalization: Charles Bertin, Susanne Lilar, Georges Sion and other Belgian playwrights have opted to write plays with no Belgium in them. In a funny way, it is also a very Belgian thing to do! One way or the other, the signature national discomfort, ever in restless quest of an elusive national identity, provides a wonderful Petrie dish for creative ferment.

# THIS IS NOT A REAL PIPE

A Philosophical Comedy

by

PASCAL VREBOS

## CAST

Jean-Jacques Hamilton, *alias* JJH, *a short, feisty, alert man in his 60s*

Mariama, *alias* Jewel, *young woman of foreign origin in her 30s*

Marianne, *aged 50, wife to* JJH

Jimmy Rockmaster, *Mariama's lawyer*

X, *spy, alias* Borderline

Pierre Yves, *international celebrity investigative reporter*

Nick, *close friend of* JJH

Helen, *undercover cop working in special operations*

Robert H. Hammond, JJH*'s lawyer*

The Whomever, *face and voice of anonymous individuals*

*Except for* JJH, *all the male characters may be played by a single actor, and the same actress may play the roles of* Marianne *and* Helen.

## SCENE ONE

*During these segments* JJH *is alone, sitting opposite an interlocutor who is never visible and who could be a shrink in a therapy session, his mother, some other person, or himself. From time to time,* HE *moves a piece on a chessboard or feverishly sends a text message.*

JJH: What the hell am I doing here? Sitting across from you? In disgrace with human society. (*Honeyed.*) Jean-Jacques Hamilton. *Enchanté*! Lovely to meet you. JJH is my world-wide brand. JJH. . . worse than Caligula, worse than Hitler. . . worse than Pinocchio! (HE *seems utterly crushed and disoriented.*) Every part of my body hurts. Is there anything you can do to ease that pain, Doctor? Have you ever experienced the worst possible bottoming out? I played and I lost, but the game never made any sense. The dice were weighted. Check and checkmate! (HE *knocks down all the chess pieces with a brutal gesture.*) I've managed to screw it up royally. (HE *laughs weirdly.*) On account of one lousy rush job fellatio incident which regaled populations all over the world! Is this session going to be over soon? Am I dreaming here? The bastards! (HE *suddenly starts imitating a monkey, uttering little cries.*) A chimpanzee in heat they said. A pervert with a thousand testicles. Ridiculous. Just look at what's become of me: A dishrag crippled with sciatica. (HE *waves in pain.*) A victim, guilty before proven guilty. (*Short silence.*) You have nothing to say. So the session's over? I'll text my wife. She's more worried than me. Well. . . to a different lady actually. Life goes on. You just cringed. Just barely, but I caught you. The eye of power. (*Short silence.*) I'm just another pathetic human entity and, in consequence, guilty. Human beings are all tailor-made for condemnation. The human being celestial? Or the human being as living crud? (HE *throws himself against wall.*) In my cell 0754-G, they ordered me to touch the wall with my nose and exit the cell backwards. I, who have set my ass down on thrones in palaces all over this lousy fucking planet! What exactly am I supposed to be accomplishing here with you anyway? Getting at the truth? My truth? The seamy residue of truth? The least false lie? The least true truth? Blahblah, blahblah! I've read and I've been hearing an endless stream of stuff. . . The hypocritical farce of the century. (HE *yells.*) The bastards! What? What's that you ask? What really happened in that hotel room on that fucking Thursday at six minutes after noon? Nothing happened, nothing. Well, almost nothing.

## SCENE TWO

*Hotel room. Several doors including one to the bathroom and to two other adjoining rooms. A sofa, a table piled high with stuff, and on the ground, an open suitcase.*

*In a symbolic separate area, as if he were commenting on the action,* JIMMY ROCKMASTER, MARIAMA's *lawyer.* JJH *and* MARIAMA *freeze whenever* HE *speaks.*

MARIAMA *enters the room and starts to tidy up, as* JJH, *naked, a towel in hand, suddenly appears facing* HER.

ROCKMASTER: There's the monster. Wearing the facial expression of a man who's used to possessing. The stance of power. The great white tycoon who has it all. . . face to face with an exotic foreigner who has nothing. Note the conqueror's body, as it instantly starts to drool over its booty. A real high-class rape. A classic, ladies and gentlemen of the jury, grounded in the most ordinary type of racism and sexism.

MARIAMA: Oh, excuse me sir. I thought you'd gone out.

JJH: I'm really and truly here. And as you can see, in tip-top shape.

ROCKMASTER: (*Aggressively.*) No, no, Mr. Hamilton, you lie. You've never been so elegant! You never are! Wherever you plant your feet, you are known for savage acts against women, for treating them as though they were merchandise, with an impunity of which you're actually proud! First you get away with murder, and then you brag about it.

MARIAMA: Oh, excuse me, sir, I thought you'd gone out.

JJH: I'm here. I'm sure you consider my dick divine. And it is about to fuck you, my beauty! (SHE *turns around and starts to leave when* JJH *grabs* HER *by the shoulders and waist.*) I wouldn't want you to have wasted your time in coming here. (HE *fondles her breasts and tries to tear off her bra, as* HE *drags* HER *into the bathroom.*) This is what you came for, you slut. You knew I was here all along.

VOICE OF MARIAMA: No, no, you're hurting me. I want to go.

VOICE OF JJH: You're a good actress. Your breasts are sizzling hot. (SHE *runs out of the bathroom and toward the door, but* HE *catches up to* HER *and locks the door.*) Fun for me. Fun for you. It's a fair deal. Thong or panties? I bet neither. A first-class hussy!

(SHE *drops to her knees virtually imploring.*)

MARIAMA: I beg of you.

JJH: (*Imitating her.*) "I beg of you." I like that. You know what it takes to get the fish to bite. Quick, spread your legs. Let's get it over with. You know who I am, don't you? You know who I am? I've had thousands of them before you, and lots more choosy than you. Don't have time to explain the concept, but you'll get a chance to test it out. (HE *laughs.*) With my testosterone. (HE *doesn't succeed in making* HER *lay down or penetrating her.*) Fine. I'll settle for your mouth, but then no orgasm for you! Get a move on. I'm already late for breakfast. (SHE *huddles on the ground, repeating* "no, no, no" *like a religious chant.*) You're doing that just to get me hot!

MARIAMA: There was nothing I could do. He threatened me. I was afraid I was going to die. I kept thinking about my daughter. (HE *pulls* HER *up against him.* SHE *mutters phrases in an unknown language.*)

JJH: Shut up! You're spoiling my concentration.

ROCKMASTER: It was pure aggression on your part, and your smutty, humiliating language. With Mariama paralyzed, Mariama stung to immobility like some animal preparing for its immolation, you crushed her head against your penis with a brutal, violent pumping motion. . . (*His voice quivering.*) In a gross, disgusting, barbaric fashion, sleazy rich guy sullying the innocent party put up for ransom by the Dominant System.

JJH: (*Sincerely.*) Did you at least get a taste of how momentous that experience was? (SHE *cries and spits on the carpet.* HE *puts his clothes back on.*) How much do you make a month? 25? 30?

ROCKMASTER: She hurt all over. Broken. Brutalized. You promised her a thousand dollars to keep her mouth shut, for you sensed, as you got dressed, that she'd been pushed too far and that she might spill the beans. . .

JJH: (*To the lawyer.*) Pure character assassination with your piddling lawyer's verbal tricks. I never paid a woman in my life! I didn't promise her a thing, and the only thing I gave her was a delicious, impromptu erotic experience.

ROCKMASTER: In the face of such villainy, of such lies, of such contempt for the law, before so many incontrovertible proofs of squalor, ladies and gentlemen of the jury, I ask you for the verdict of guilty of rape and abduction by force. . . Let this wretched creature finish out his days in prison. Prevent him from ever again backsliding. Think of your own daughter or your wife, who might some day be his next victims.

JJH: (*To* MARIAMA, *as* SHE *gets up.*) My tie! Where did I stick my tie? Did you take it as a trophy? Give it back. It's a present from my daughter. It's an Armani. If you like, you can have this pair of socks as a souvenir. And pack my suitcase. Get a move on! You made me late.

## SCENE THREE

JJH *again alone as in Scene One.*

JJH: I really don't give a damn whether I talk to you or not after that business. I've never talked about myself in that way. I'm just a poor slob. Well, poor in the metaphysical sense of the word, a poor schlep. You know.

*Silence.* HE *moves a piece on the chessboard.*

My wife's made of money, and I've cheated on her left, right, and center with an admirable fidelity. I did it because I loved her. . . and because she never deserved to be the endless butt of all my inexhaustible grungy impulses. But just try explaining that to all the dunces on this uptight planet, conditioned as they are to live by a morality fit only for slaves! I'd consider spitting out this universal truth in a public forum, but then it'd be the guillotine for me. (HE *laughs and sends a text.*) And you, who are you? A real shrink? Or some kind of secret agent working for you know who? What? You're waiting for me to confess to something more intimate. (*Ironically.*) I've done nothing *but* strip myself naked before you since I got here, divulging all my inside scoops and dark corners. . .

*Silence.*

The first time. You're really into those, aren't you? First times. They mark you for life. Fourteen years old.

*Silence.*

You remember that tall friend of yours, mama, Corinne. . . ? A beautiful woman. She walked into my bedroom looking for God knows what. . .

and there. . . in the gloom of a hot summer day and divinely cool sheets. . . (*Short silence.*) A burbling-up of the being. A spewing forth of all the senses. Never experienced that again. So what if ever since all I've been doing is to desperately try and relive that one Big Bang? Are you satisfied, Doctor? Are you feeling any stirrings of love for JJH, like all the rest?

## SCENE FOUR

MARIANNE *is discovered in the separate area.*

MARIANNE: (*Calm, serene.*) My husband is an exceptional being, gifted in all ways, with a fiery temperament. He's a poet of daily life who's preserved his childlike side and his untamed side, which causes great men the world over to get in line. He casts a new light on all he sees.

JJH, *naked, comes out of the bathroom with a towel around his neck to find himself nose to nose with* MARIAMA. JJH *pulls back in surprise.* MARIAMA *smiles.*

JJH: Sorry. Would you mind passing me my dressing gown?

MARIAMA: (*While picking up his dressing gown extremely slowly and holding it in her hands.*) Nudity doesn't bother me. You're a handsome man, just the way I like them. Wide, solid, with a hairy chest, a glint in his eye. The face of a man born to lead.

JJH: Pass me my dressing gown please.

MARIAMA: (*Laughing.*) I see I'm making a certain impact on you.

JJH: You're nice, but I'm in a hurry. I've got business to see to.

MARIAMA: And my business is you. I find you attractive. I like the unexpected. Back home, where I come from, pleasure is king.

SHE *throws the dressing gown far off.*

MARIANNE: (*Angrily.*) Everything they're all saying is nothing but filthy libel. My husband is incapable of so much as the slightest drop of violence. Even a mosquito he's incapable of crushing. That woman—it's entrapment pure and simple. All the women run after him. It's his charm, his position.

Power draws women the way slime draws cockroaches. The poor man spends all his time saying no, but sometimes he folds. There've been times I've folded too. So what? That's life. A little beddy-bye, some wham-bam, thank you ma'am, a drop of mucal fluid exchange, no big deal. (*Tenderly.*) You know, I love you. . . almost the same as at the very start.

JJH: Me too my love. You know that. My life began when you came into my life. . .

MARIAMA: You've never made love with a woman like me.

JJH: Oh yes I have. . . If you only knew—back in my country I'm a total libertine. I'm not straitlaced, not prudish.

MARIAMA: Libertine? Prudish. You use such high-sounding words in a manner so rudish. So you're a puritan like the Americans?

JJH: No, just the opposite.

MARIAMA: So?! You know, when it comes to men, I'm pretty hard to please. But you're handsome and strong. (SHE *reads his palm.*) And generous.

SHE *has taken off her blouse and slipped off her skirt, caresses his torso and kisses him.*

MARIANNE: Get your clothes back on, you bitch! Get out of there! You'll be the death of him. You're going to feed him to the wolves!

JJH: Some other time, but at the moment it's just not possible. I'm pressed for time.

MARIANNE: He said no. And for him, that really takes a considerable effort.

MARIAMA: Your peepee says yes.

JJH: He always says yes.

MARIAMA: No one will say a word. Nobody will ever know. It'll be our secret.

MARIANNE: How could he resist? What man could turn down such a temptation? She was angling for cash, that whore, and he didn't give her any. He believed she really desired him. Like all men. My husband is innocent. (*Practically yelling.*) Innocent!

JJH: (*Getting dressed.*) You really came here by accident?

MARIAMA: Accident is never an accident. That's a saying of my people.

JJH: Did Jimmy send you?

MARIAMA: (*Laughing ambiguously.*) I came because I came.

JJH: A nice little present to myself before taking the great plunge into the upcoming election.

## SCENE FIVE

JJH, *alone once more.*

JJH: (*Furious, pacing the stage, intermittently staring at his imaginary interlocutor, at times falling into the cliché walk of someone under criminal suspicion.*) Do you hold it against me that I was exhibited before all the world handcuffed like some little nobody? Guilty by justice-fiction! But guilty of what?

HE *strings together long choppy phrases.*

A poor petty precipitate . . . non-erotically correct *prejudiced* blow-job, one non-jurisprudently adequate. . . one *presumedly* un-reciprocal. . . a world renowned blowjob. . . an act of fellatio gone over with a fine-toothed comb by the populations of all nations, that is where we now stand! The world's heading for total collapse, financiers are diddling with the neutron bomb, we're rapidly approaching the sixth extinction of the species, and lo and behold, the entire planet accuses the insatiable satyr of the crime—at my age, mind you—of orgasm without spermission!

HE *snickers. Short silence.* HE *sends a text.*

If you compare me to the rest of the history of sexuality, I'm practically a saint. And you know it too, Doctor. You who've made a study of the full gamut of human experimentation! Who am I compared to Tiberius who had himself sucked off by new-born babies, the *fellator verpae*, as they called him. Tiberius: guilty as charged! All those men, and all those women . . . in ancient times combined to form endless chains with animals, the chug-chug of orgasm! Guilty as charged! And at Pompei, where there were more bordellos than bakeshops, there too, they treated themselves to it and how! Guilty as charged! And how about the saying of Theodora, mistress of Justinian. . . "I employ the three orifices of my body," she sang, "but why oh why didn't nature see fit to poke holes in my breasts as well?" Guilty! Into the hole! Into the cell! Death to her!

HE *seems exhausted, breathes with difficulty.* HE *moves a chess piece.*

If my wife—who by the way is no doormat, but one half of a couple—has forgiven me for this massacre they've made out of a molehill, then why can't the rest of the planet? I am a victim of my own libido. (*Dreamily.*) Clinton got off lighter for his Monica than I did for my Mariama. . .

## SCENE SIX

BORDERLINE, *a sort of high-strung special agent who wishes to remain anonymous, is discovered in the separate area.*

HE *is watching* MARIAMA *methodically foraging through* JJH*'s stuff.* SHE *picks out a datebook that* SHE *hides beneath her skirt.*

BORDERLINE: A real pro. The way she ferrets through stuff. Top-notch training. Can't help but admire her classiness. I know my job through and through. I bust my ass on all the trickiest cases. I'm always on the edge. And that's why I'm known as Borderline. (HE *laughs mechanically.*)

SHE *is going through the suitcase when* JJH *suddenly bursts out of the bathroom wearing his dressing gown.*

JJH: What are you doing here?

MARIAMA: I'm straightening up your room, sir. Excuse me. They told me you'd left.

JJH: I am leaving. I was just about to check out of this hotel.

MARIAMA: I'll be going.

SHE *turns around, bends over, and picks up a pair of socks.*

JJH: (*Laughing.*) Hey, you're not wearing any underwear.

BORDERLINE: A real pro, like I told you. In case of unexpected glitch in this sort of caper, a sex gambit always comes in handy. Power is an invitation to sex. And everyone's got this bird's number. A crack-brained chump, no doubt about it. He was bound to be put out of his misery sooner or later. This operation'll have to be paired up with another. Kind of "Sensitive Documents" or "Sex Team" jobbie. Whole thing's captured on video. Reminds me of the Clinton caper. I bet, at the end of the day, they come up with nothing but pigeon semen on her skirt. All of a sudden she's got company. Two agents in the hallway and two in the room next door. Every eventuality has been taken into account. And it's all being monitored in real time, at the very highest levels.

MARIAMA: I never wear any.

JJH: (*Approaching her.*) Just like in porn films.

MARIAM: I've acted in those just to top off my monthly salary. I like doing it. And you?

JJH: I love life.

BORDERLINE: You saw the whole thing right before your very eyes. She segues right into the sex gambit, all the while looking for the guy's cell-phone. And in her right shoe there's a little white weapon. If things go south she won't hesitate to use it. She'll bleed him dry. I've had a look at the notes. Shooting all the broads on sight isn't enough for this guy. He's so full of himself, he's oblivious to the most obvious things. He even tried to take on white-collar crime and change the monetary standard of the dollar!

JJH: (*Who has closed in on her.*) I love life, so I like the pleasures of the senses. (HE *caresses her breasts.*) In all places and in all positions.

MARIAMA: For my sins, take me doggy style if you feel like it, or the missionary position right here on the carpet, or the "Union of the Octopus." That's my signature kama-sutra specialty.

JJH: (*Smiling.*) You epitomize the expert chamber-maid beautifully. That Octopus sure sounds tempting. Never heard of it before now. Last month I spent a lot of time practicing "The Galloping Andromache."

MARIAMA: I know that one too. Let's give Andromache a shot!

JJH: (*Regretfully.*) Don't have time for it. . .

MARIAMA: (*Laughing and caressing him.*) Get a move on! Gallop!

JJH: I really have to go. . . but your lovely mouth. . .

BORDERLINE: There. Operation almost in the bag. She's located the cell-phone. Once the tasty treat's over and done with, she'll grab it. Clean job. Didn't have to wade too deep into the slime-pit. The guy's goose is cooked. Cooked to a turn.

## SCENE SEVEN

JJH *again alone.*

HE *is immobile before his game of chess and stares fixedly at his imaginary interlocutor.*

JJH: Whatever are we going to do about the planet? Whatever are we going to do about our species? I had a plan. A type of megalomaniacal master plan. Right on the level with who I am: A plan for getting this society, that's hurtling toward the abyss, back on track. (HE *moves a chess piece.*) Neutralize all the crazies who are rotting out the works of the Machine, and replace the engineering of finance with an engineering of survival. A grand scheme! Revolutionary, intelligent and pragmatic. Made in my own image. And now I've been portrayed as some kind of mental deviant.

HE *contorts his body, sticks out his tongue, makes obscene gestures.*

(*Depressed.*) The Titanic Syndrome. The ship's leaking and everyone just keeps shimmying on the deck. I'm serious though. None of the famous Rating Agencies ever warned of the slightest little financial crisis. They didn't care to let it be known that a debacle was on the way. Hush-hush, the stock exchange brought low by an unimpeded fluid exchange of un-unloadable contaminated purchases, the sacred chain of moolah! Oh no! Credit's the semen which impregnates the economy. I'll stop. I see that this doesn't interest you. You'd much rather I go on about my sexual contortions. They're less subversive. . . My downfall delighted all the Ebenezer Scrooges of the world. They will go right on amassing, possessing more and more, all the better to wind up possessed themselves.

*Short silence.*

Yes, I know, I can see you coming with your big clodhoppers, even I. . . As a result of possessing all those women, I wind up. . . possessed by them. Her! Her! Ideal place to weigh anchor, ideal place to drill. . . (*Softly.*) I'm lost when I think of them all. (*Like a child.*) At a loss before so many curves, folds, shadows, orifices. . . from which I come, from which you come, and which is the game of death.

*Short silence.*

(*Like a howl.*) Mariama was a consenting adult.

## SCENE EIGHT

PIERRE YVES, *international celebrity investigative reporter, is discovered in the separate area.*

MARIAMA *is seen in the room, perfectly relaxed, smoking a cigarette and distractedly arranging* JJH*'s stuff.* SHE *removes her blouse.* JJH *comes out of the bathroom wearing his dressing gown.*

JJH: I didn't hear you come in, my Jewel.

MARIAMA: Always discreet. . . And I wanted you to surprise me naked!

JJH: Okay, I'll go back into the bathroom.

MARIAMA: (*Continuing to undress.*) I don't like that look on your face.

VOICE OF JJH: Too much stress, too much work, too much too much. The election. (HE *pokes his head out. With a drop of irony.*) The weight of the world. You are resplendent.

MARIAMA: Whenever you're around I sparkle. When I'm vacuuming, my light goes out.

JJH: (*Coming out.*) I'm pressed for time today. I'm having lunch with my daughter, and then, I've got to race to the airport.

MARIAMA: (*Wrapping him in her arm.*) You've been pressed for time ever since I've known you. Except for one particular time.

JJH: That Thanksgiving two years ago!

MARIAMA: (*Touched.*) The turkey in the bedroom, and then one whole night! What are you up for?

JJH: Something quick and good.

MARIAMA: Code 12, I bet.

JJH: Code 12 it is!

SHE *pulls him into the bathroom.*

PIERRE YVES: I'm starting to get a strong feeling that they know each other. A relationship dating back several years. Intermittent episodes in the same hotel where Mariama works half-time. I've put together a list of his regular women the world over. Information checked and double-checked. Nothing illegal. Anyway, you know you can always find a few fleas on that kind of camel. Tatiana, Moscow. Irina, Kiev. Raluca, Bucharest. Poppi, Athens. Christine, Brussels. Fang, Peking. Annemie, The Hague. Antoinette, Quebec. Manuela, La Paz. Antonella, Rome. Greta, Stockholm. Ayla, Istanbul. Cindy, London. Emerancy, Kinshasa. . . and those are just the ones I've managed to lay my hands on.

JJH *and* MARIAMA *come out of the bathroom.*

MARIAMA: Six minutes flat!

SHE *is wiping her mouth with a tissue.*

JJH: But what delicious minutes they were!

MARIAMA: You got it all over me. When do you get back?

JJH: (*While getting dressed and closing his suitcase.*) I don't know.

MARIAMA: Next month?

JJH: Listen, I've got something to say to you that I don't enjoy having to say. We're not going to see each other again.

MARIAMA: (*Speechless.*) Why?

JJH: They're hot on my trail. The elections're coming up. Too risky. Too many responsibilities.

MARIAMA: And what am I supposed to do without you?

JJH: (*Pragmatic and cold.*) Someone will be sending you money for the upkeep of your daughter, have no fear. Nothing will be any different.

MARIAMA: (*Angrily.*) Everything will be different! I don't want it to change.

JJH: I'm very sorry Jewel.

MARIAMA: (*Yelling.*) Sorry?! You throw me out like a kleenex with a tiny little check every month. I'm not a whore. If you dismiss me, you're going to really have to cough up! You can take your change-purse and stuff it! You're a real bastard! But I've got photos of us. I can blackmail you, and I want plenty! A truckload of cash! (SHE *cries.*) I love you, I do. I love you, don't you get it?

JJH: No, I don't get it. I like you for your ass, and that's all.

MARIAMA: (*Sobbing.*) It is not all. I love you! I, I love you!

PIERRE YVES: She clings to him. She wasn't expecting this rupture. And he, he is struck dumb. He keeps the word "love" in reserve exclusively for his wife. He keeps looking at his watch. In any case, he's off somewhere. This scene exasperates him, and not for one second does he imagine that Mariama is actually hurt. It would have been an incredible scoop, but my editor-in-chief wanted no part of it, not even that amazing list. No need to ask what kind of screws were being put to him. All that work for nothing. Unless I try to sell it elsewhere. . .

MARIAMA: I love you. How about you?

JJH: I appreciate you enormously. But. . .

MARIAMA: But what? We could see each other from time to time. We could do it in secret.

JJH: (*Icy.*) We'll never see each other again.

MARIAMA: (*Beating up on him.*) You'll pay for that.

## SCENE NINE

JJH *is again alone.*

JJH: Who am I? (HE *shrugs*) I'm the collateral damage from a drop of destiny's drool. Nice, hunh? (HE *moves a chess piece*). But that does nothing to advance our game. Who am I? My mother loved me. My father doted on me. I had every privilege under the sun. I went into the cupboard to steal chocolates. I staged tantrums when it didn't turn out the way I wanted. *Oh, you darling boy!* I lied like all bald-faced liars. I was the center of the universe. *Oh, you darling boy.* Mama, you see where your undying love has got us? The truth is a main course. . . garnished with a tangle of lies. Mine is, in any case. Yours too. There's a marvelous truth socked away inside any lie. Nice, isn't it? I'm a walking void. An arranger of packs of verities. Power demands it. To survive. To keep hold of it. To reinforce it. Read your Shakespeare. Read your Machiavelli. If you call it for what it is, the people will chop your head off, and your competitors will steal your place out from under you. And that's why the powerful of the world are apt to lie as soon as breathe. And they're not the only ones. Broadcasters just the same. Those clowns rattle off whatever they feel like. Dance around in plain sight, spout whatever their clients want you to hear. Poor little pygmies that they are; imagining they're titans. I've always held them in total contempt, but that hasn't stopped me from kissing their asses on occasion or taking them out to three-star restaurants. I'm such a bullshit artist. Even I can get it wrong. When I was in prison I wanted to kill myself. The fluorescent lights. The moldy walls. The black soap and those coarse towels. The slamming of the iron doors. But I had nothing to do it with. Not even a tiny blade to stick the supposed pig they were trying to make me into. That's a lie. I'm too scared of death. To be no more—it's abominable, atrocious, even if you're not around to know it. The dread of death can drive a person crazy and make him capable of anything! What if that was the key, Doctor? When I was little I was immortal, all-powerful. I *want*, I *want*, and I *got*. Got is a thing of the past. I've got nothing. Nothing left. What's the point? Nothing? That's the truth of the matter. You know what? I'm not a Casanova. The only way I can get it up's with Viagra.

## SCENE TEN

NICK, *close friend of* JJH, *is discovered in the special area.*

NICK: I know Jean-Jacques as though I'd created him myself. From way back in elementary school, and we've been inseparable every since. I've read everything written about that mess, and we've been over the whole thing together. They've done in an innocent man. The Jean-Jacques I know is tender and kind. A superior man from every point of view. Generous, funny. Sure, I know he's hot to trot. Well—sizzling hot to trot, maybe. But so romantic, crazy about the ladies, and especially his own particular one. In reality he's a knight out to conquer, on an initiatic quest for the Feminine Principle, seeking some hyper-concentrated concept of Woman. He's a regular platonic philosopher for Christ's sake! It's true, sometimes yes, when they've got a virile personality like him, platonic philosophers don't necessarily act all that platonically. . . And besides, fate can always come knocking at a bedroom door. There she is. There she is. A woman of ebony. A gift from heaven or. . . from hell.

MARIAMA *enters with a vacuum cleaner.* JJH *comes out of the bathroom, naked from behind.*

MARIAMA: Oh, I'm so sorry. Sorry, sir. I must have stepped into the wrong room. . .

JJH: A beauty like you is never wrong. Heaven sent you to me.

MARIAMA: Excuse me yet again, sir.

JJH: Not so fast. You're an angel! (*With a tender, gentle voice.*) You have bewitchingly delicate eyes. And the eyes are the antechamber which leads to the heart and the soul. Your eyes shine like a diamond, through which one can glean a shimmering sea.

NICK: You systematically wrapped them up in words. I always wondered where you got them from.

JJH: I know loads of sonnets by heart. Women have need of poetry, Nick. It's a lubricant for the soul! Before you screw them it's a good idea to spout a stream of romantic poetry.

NICK: It's true. Even with encounters at the very summit, with extremely powerful women, he'd quote Victor Hugo or Louis Aragon, and the negotiations would start tilting in his favor.

JJH: (*to* MARIAMA.) You're an angel with wildly curvaceous legs that waft you from room to room. . .

MARIAMA: Now you're going too far. . .

JJH: You're a divine beauty casting its divine light on me, and see how, even in my nudity, I step down off my pedestal to address you as the essence of Beauty itself! I am in the same position as Adam, and you, 'ere long, of Eve!

MARIAMA: No man has ever spoken to me like that. . .

JJH: If I was a bumblebee and you, a flower, I'd pass all my days ravishing your heart, and . . . everything else too.

MARIAMA: (*Smiling.*) You're off your rocker!

JJH: Every cell in my skin quivers at the promise of such a sweet body as yours. For me, you've burst into my life like the sun through these sad gray days. Answer me, my angel. I need you so desperately. It's all I'll ever ask for—just a tiny bit of you. . .

MARIAMA: You speak well to ladies. But I must admit that I haven't understood it all.

JJH: (*Brusquely.*) Shit! So I said all that stuff for nothing!? Look, lose that vacuum cleaner, and let's get a move on. Are you in the mood or not?

MARIAMA: (*Still smiling.*) But surely you have a job and a wife.

JJH: But I've also got problems galore. Stress night and day. And you, there you are like an offering I never would have expected again in life. My Eve, for just a moment, I shall adorn you with kisses and diamonds.

MARIAMA: Are you a diamond dealer?

JJH: (*Slightly exasperated.*) The diamonds were just an image, but I've got plenty of kisses and to spare.

MARIAMA: You're very nice. You talk like a book. You're charming. Yes, you've got a great deal of charm. But my boss is going to beep me any minute now.

JJH: Who cares? Do you know who I am? Nobody's ever dared to beep me! Enough chit-chat. I've got an airplane to catch. I bet you're hot. Let's fuck now. (*He wraps his arms around her.*) What's your name?

MARIAMA: Jewel. But. . .

JJH: (*Interrupting her.*) I might have known. You're the most beautiful thing I've ever held in my arms.

*Blackout on* THE COUPLE.

NICK: Dotty as he is, I never fail to imagine him in the arms of Venus. Words that caress. His look that can tear at your heartstrings. He hasn't gotten where he is by accident.

*Lights up on* THE COUPLE.

JJH: Sorry. I came like a teenager. I couldn't help it. Let me give your shirt a wipe.

MARIAMA: (*Disconcerted.*) Leave it. It'll be a souvenir. An amazing souvenir.

JJH: Pure pleasure.

MARIAMA: What's your name? And who do you think you are that you believe you can do whatever you feel like?

JJH: (*Laughing.*) Jean-Jacques, and I'm practically Master of the Universe.

NICK: In a word, feel free to write it down and to quote me. What started off as a delightful French farce segued into a bloodbath.

## SCENE ELEVEN

JJH *is alone and says nothing to his imaginary interlocutor.*

JJH: *(After a moment.)* You're getting on my last nerve. What is it you're waiting for? Oh, yes—I'm here to tell you about the Thing. Those silences of yours unhinge me. I'm incorrigible. (HE *yells.*) I'm an ejaculator. *(Ironically.)* Take note, take careful note—that's a neurosis that hasn't been given a clinical classification yet. I ejaculate the way others guzzle whiskey or chain smoke. But I'm an un-solitary ejaculator. There've got to be two involved at the very least, or else it's of no interest to me. So is it a personality disorder or was I just gifted from birth? What man wouldn't dream of being a King Kong of the pillows? Anything with mucous inside is miraculous, no matter if its owner be brunettish, blondish, a novice, an old biddy, a model, handicapped (I champion all kinds of anti-discrimination causes!). Just so long as I get to spermalate in the end, and the material in question gets to have their own orgasm as well. Each new episode is a finely calculated risk. Just have to make sure that the warehouse is fully stocked so I can dip back into the merchandise as need dictates. But ever since I was a small child and escaped from a fire I believe I've had luck on my side! Invincible! Untouchable! I'm always ready to pounce. What is it you want me to show you, Doctor? (HE *mimes the scene.*) I walk into a meeting. Shake hands and drop some extremely profound banalities, all the while sweeping the room with a circular laser survey. Like that. . . And once I single one out, I fix her with a Mona Lisa smile, an insistent stare, and after the look has been applied, I then move on to another. From bottom to top, I scan her insistently. I wind up for the pitch, she blushes, intrigued, at which point I go over to her. I grab and hold onto her hand longer than is customary. I murmur, "I want you. You're already practically mine." Which generally yields a 50% success rate. The other 50% I send them hundreds of texts, and 25% wind up accepting, especially the married women, Doctor, and a certain number have actually put an end to their lives because *I've* put an end to *it*. Why don't you pipe up? Jealous? You find it amusing, hunh, all this lubricating jelly and secretions emitted from our rational animal parts.

*Short silence.*

Does anyone out there know how it actually all works? In this chess match. . . (HE *moves two pawns.*) One pawn to the left, one pawn to the right. . . thousands over here, thousands over there, you pretend you're totally on top of things, while in point of fact, you're improvising the whole time. Some amass their dollars under the sign of the golden calf. Others—far more numerous—die of starvation, their throats dry, and the smell of death just a tip left on the table. And then there's me, on this shit-pile I'm forever scaling—when all I ever really want to do is cum. What's so terrible about that? (*Softly.*) I do what I can. I'm not all that successful. I make myself seem interesting. I schmooze, I blab. I panic. Scared of my own shadow. Get it back under wraps. So then go back to swaggering. Peacocking around.

*Short silence.*

I'm four years old. I think I'm going to die. There in that gummy smoke, the flames gobbling up the ceiling, the taste of cinders in my mouth, the boys and girls, all friends I can no longer see, enveloped in smoke, fire shooting out of them as they howl in pain. . . I have no idea how I ever got out of there, but I did. . . So it's best to cum before you die. Cum, cum, (*Getting carried away.*) cum, cum, cum, cum, cum! (*Suddenly calming down.*) A pretty picture, isn't it?

## SCENE TWELVE

HELEN, *undercover cop, specialist in extra covert operations, is discovered in the separate area.*

*The doorbell rings in the hotel room.* JJH *comes out in his dressing gown and goes to open the door, welcoming* MARIAMA.

JJH: Delighted, miss.

MARIAMA: Call me Mariama or Jewel. Jewel is for my intimate friends.

JJH: (*Laughing.*) Then it'll have to be Jewel.

MARIAMA: (*In consternation.*) If it has to be, then it has to.

JJH: Take a seat. Relax. (*Looking at his watch.*) We've got some time.

MARIAMA: Even so, you're so impressive, and I've got the willies.

JJH: They won't last. "You know who" surely explained everything to you. He leaves no stone unturned.

MARIAMA: Yes, yes, and I signed. Look.

SHE *hands him a piece of paper that* HE *scans distractedly.*

JJH: Will you be able to stick with it for the long haul? There's going to be a lot of shaking up. There's going to be a lot of hard slapping-around.

MARIAMA: I prepared myself. In my head especially. And for you it'll be even more horrible, won't it?

JJH: In the beginning, yes. The horror, the unrelenting attack, the torture. But after. . . (HE *breathes voluptuously.*)

MARIAMA: May I confess something?

JJH: I know all about you. You are discrete and deserving. No illegal acts—well, none except the ones that work for us. No drugs. . . and a past that'd make their heartstrings throb.

MARIAMA: One question then: why do you want to lose everything? I'd like to know.

HELEN: (*Holding up her I.D. card.*) Helen, special agent. . . From a criminal justice standpoint, a hotel maid is the ultimate cover. You can rifle through things at your leisure, you can requisition things without a search warrant. No one suspects you, and you're a woman to boot. And I stumbled onto this whole affair totally by accident while I was on the trail of a diplomat involved in human organ traffic! JJH is paying the price for his descent into hell, I feel quite sure, just so he can get some peace in his life. He set the whole thing up. He couldn't be higher up on the food chain, and he'd have had to fight to climb any higher. So he cooked up a nice horror film just so's he could slip out a back door. Is that the reaction of a manic-depressive? Or is it a bet placed by an egocentric gambler? One thing's for sure: He's a wild card and everyone's going to fall right into his trap.

MARIAMA: But why give up everything you have? I'd like to know.

JJH: Tranquility, serenity, freedom are priceless. (*Smiling.*) And later, much, much later, I'll write a book and no one will believe it.

MARIAMA: But you're one of the most powerful men on the planet, and tomorrow after this you'll be nothing.

JJH: Not nothing! Less than nothing! Demolished! A pervert! A low-life! A shit! I'll be swept up in a torrent of insanity. My friends will hold their noses, the media will be all over it, selling their images and their toilet paper as usual. . . Everyone'll be running away from me except for a select few. The real ones. I've had it up to here with this pseudo-elite that's dragging the world right to kingdom-come. The daily whirlpool with its social charades and the puppets who've been put in office by all the zombies. Financiers who the only thing they finance is themselves.

MARIAMA: But your wife is crazy about you. "You know who" told me.

JJH: She's lost the ability to understand me. Those days are over. And my feelings no longer chime with hers. That's how it is. But why am telling you all this?

MARIAMA: (*Tenderly.*) Because we're accomplices. And because I'll be a million dollar tombstone for you.

JJH: You'll see. You'll earn your keep.

*Telephone rings.*

MARIANNE: Is everything alright dear?

JJH: Yes, dear, I'm just packing my suitcase.

MARIANNE: "Don't forget the acacia and the purloined ladybugs in your suitcase."

JJH: No, no, and "The snakes from the Eiffel Tower are still chewing our old bougainvilleas and fig jam." Here's a kiss for you. I love you. See you tomorrow.

MARIAMA: You play your part very well.

JJH: It's a secret code, since they're always listening in. I'm being bugged. It's a habit.

MARIAMA: "I love you. See you tomorrow. . ."

JJH: It's my inner chameleon. Okay. It's not that I'm not enjoying our conversation, but it's high time we get moving. Action!

HE *takes out a flask and hands it to* HER.

HELEN: In that flask there is semen. She's going to smear it all over her skirt and onto the carpet. They won't know what hit them. (SHE *chuckles.*) When it comes to matters where expertise is called for, the experts are often wrong. My report's been shredded. They ordered me to close the case and granted me three months paid vacation, beach chair and umbrellas included.

MARIAMA: If you'd rather, I could do it for real. (SHE *laughs.*) It'll be included in the price.

JJH: That's a nice idea, but I just made love with a friend of mine, and my reputation for multiple orgasms is greatly exaggerated.

SHE *pours a little semen on her skirt and onto the carpet.*

JJH: (*Opening his dressing gown.*) A few nail marks here too. Yes, on my chest. The D.N.A. crew just adores that. (SHE *scratches him, laughing.*)

MARIAMA: You're my very own Santa Claus.

JJH: Thank you for everything, Jewel, and I wish you a wonderful life.

*SHE kisses him on both cheeks.*

## SCENE THIRTEEN

HE *is again alone, facing his interlocutor.*

*His voice, his body language, his gestures are mercurial, sometimes quite disturbingly so.*

JJH: (*Starts humming in a totally unexpected manner, atypical of his personality.*)
At twilight
I ejaculate through my stamen.
Shoot my way through the dawn's early light.
Activate vesicles.
A summer sperm festival!
Press on o testicles!
A genuine caveman.

When I cum
A whole chest-full!

The hit song of the summer about the torments of getting it on! Humanity's original sin. . . Eve's the one who ate the apple, not me! While I, every day of my life, I was surrounded by serpents! Billions they embezzle, and wind up getting a medal of honor! A little semen on some skirt, and it's straight to prison! Without the slightest proof! Suspicions! Hair-brained notions! (HIS *voice trembling.*) That's it. I'm done for. You've won. I wish I could cry. I never cry. Can't summon it up. Not even lemons can make me. Except for when I'm laughing and can't stop. But that's a shortcut tactic—laughing until you cry. I'll confess to whatever you want. I can't take it anymore. I want to sleep. I want to be back with my mother, my father, in the leafy garden embalming the pine trees. . . that universe where nothing under that starry vault could ever get me. (*After a silence* HE *moves a chess piece.)* For a shrink you play pretty bad. The game goes on. My wife always told me: You've got the hide of an elephant. (*Cynically.*) Come to think of it, a little late in the day, I should just have gotten hold of a prescription to hire a sex nurse for people with disabilities like mine. Night and day, she could have relieved my scrotum, getting me to cum by massaging and draining my absolutely sensational nut-sack! (*After a short silence, speaking slowly.*) I stuff myself with testosterone and nobody knows it.

*Silence.*

If not for those molecules
I wouldn't be scrounging for ovules. . .

What's that? They blame me for being direct with the ladies, jump right into action, foreskin back, making straight for where I'm aiming, penis lying there panting in a swirl of sperm. So what? Chaste kings are boring. You can't have impotent people in power. Alright, so I objectified women a little at times, same way society standardizes humans. So? Does that mean I deserve to be castrated? Nailed? Set fire to my phallus in real time on television? Guillotine my prostate under the Big Clock on Times Square at the climax of the show—the JJH Saga? What's that? Morality? Morality's for the humbled masses, for the sterile, for all the ball-less wonders. Morality doesn't exist. It's sex and its guard-dogs that brought it into being over the course of history. We're all beasts of desire, whether you like it or not. It's that pompous, frustrated flock of moralists, theologians and shrinks who invented Good Manners in order to deny and medicalize sexuality. And you're just like them—a real bastard! Sex's got nothing to do with love. You think the shepherd who humps his goat's going to write a love poem in its honor? Love was an invention, but not desire! Nature is just plain horniness and *coitus* for the sake of survival of the species. In me everything is animal, vegetable, and mineral. I'm the residual dust of the universe. . . and so they're sweeping me right off to hell. (HE *moves a pawn, smiling.*) Check to your queen! (*A silence.*) I thought that all women loved me, and that that was what they couldn't stand about me. I never believed in myself. I only pretended to. I was playing their game. (HE *moves a pawn with rage.*) Check to your king! Get me out of here Mommy! You're the one who got me into this mess in the first place.

## SCENE FOURTEEN

ROBERT H. HAMMOND, JJH*'s lawyer, is in the separate area. At certain moments,* HE *argues the case as though* HE *were in front of a jury, same as* MARIAMA'S LAWYER *did in Scene 2.*

HAMMOND: My client is an exceptional man whom they have—and I choose my words advisedly—crucified on the cross of the police, on the cross of the law, and on the cross of the media. What happened that particular Thursday at six minutes past noon in room number 7001 was the most ordinary of abbreviated sexual encounters between two consenting adults. All the rest is nothing but a fiction and manipulation of the lowest order. Odious tittle-tattle either for the sake of pecuniary gain on the part of certain amateurs or potentially a conspiracy on a higher level, but that is for the real experts to determine.

MARIAMA *is in the hotel room.* SHE *starts clearing the breakfast paraphernalia from the table.* JJH *comes out of the bathroom, half-naked.*

MARIAMA: Excuse me, excuse me. I thought that. . .

JJH: (*Interrupting, all smiles.*) You thought that I was here!

MARIAMA: No, no, not at all. I'll be going. . .

JJH: Oh, no need to hurry off.

HAMMOND: She's there. He's there. She looks at him. He perceives a slight smile. She doesn't move a muscle. My client, who likes women, in all simplicity, in all naïveté, assumes that a form of invitation has been extended.

JJH: No need to run off.

HAMMOND: She doesn't leave. She keeps looking at him.

JJH: I sense that there's something passing between us.

MARIAMA: It's against the rules. I can't stay.

JJH: Just a few minutes. Your mouth is a vision. Has anyone told you that before?

MARIAMA: I've been told.

HAMMOND: Can you believe, you, the ladies of the jury, that a woman with a build like that, one that is in point of fact manly, could actually be forced to perform fellatio on a man who is over 60 years of age and less powerfully built than she? Has Mariama lost all her teeth? Is it that Mariama's handicapped in her canines? Mutilated in her incisors? Her entire dental apparatus impaired? A young woman paralyzed by fear? Standing before this white-haired old man—study him well ladies—would you be scared of that man? Of a man of such distinction? With all that French gallantry? At one and the same time so roguish and so refined? Would you be afraid of a man whose criminal record is white as driven snow? Could you imagine that that man—as my learned colleague has dared to assert—in an odious delirium, imagine him, even for one second, making a rush at her, ravishing her body with the savagery of a semi-professional rapist, and so taking possession of the plaintiff's breasts and vagina? And the ultimate proof: there is not one iota of evidence that violence was practiced on her person. Did perhaps JJH put on gloves? You'd imagine, would you not, that the merest little trace of D.N.A. would have brought joy to the prosecuting attorney's heart, but nothing of the kind! The plaintiff is a liar, an opportunist with a dubious past, and a slut into the bargain. But I have no desire to shower her with invective, for I know all too well the kind of life this type of woman leads: fleeing poverty, they land in our pulsating metropolises and find themselves constrained to take up a life of occasional prostitution just to survive, at times via networks that are under the distant control of the murky Mafiosi of Capitalism. . . the very same networks that Jean-Jacques Hamilton was so valiantly intent on obliterating. By arresting my client in such an unjust manner—he who never raped a soul in his life—it is you, you who have raped History, for he surely will go down in History, now forever after indelibly branded as such!

MARIANNE: He pled the case fabulously my darling. The cause isn't lost. History will just have to wait a few more months for you to take your place in it.

JJH: (*As before, laughing.*) Is it actually me they're going on about? (*To* MARIANNE.) What if we opened a peaceful little bar in a glade, on a rocky promontory in Guadeloupe, nowhere remotely close to History, but someplace tranquil, oh so tranquil!

MARIANNE: No, you are an exceptional man, and you have a destiny to fulfill.

JJH: (*Again to* MARIAMA.) And I could tell that you find me attractive. From the day I was born, it's been my good fortune that women have found me attractive. Since we started talking, your pupils have gotten slightly dilated. That's a sign.

MARIAMA: (*Gently ironic.*) You have good eyesight.

JJH: Your eyes are gleaming.

MARIAMA: A little touch of allergy is all. Dust mites.

JJH: You're lying.

MARIAMA: Yes, I was lying, sort of the same way you were.

JJH: Let's convert this chance meeting into a most agreeable idyll. And from my end, the last form of recreation I'll be having for a long time.

MARIAMA: From your end, at least, you know what you want.

JJH: I've always gotten what I wanted.

MARIAMA: And what is it you do in life, apart from coming on to women?

JJH: I bring people together who hate each other. (HE *goes over to* HER.) How can I resist an apparition as delectable and unexpected as you?

MARIAMA: Are you married?

JJH: To a woman I love. But you, you I desire. . . ardently!

MARIANA: (*Mocking.*) That's what they all say.

HAMMOND: There you have the most ordinary of verbal exchanges, which as the conversation proceeds, will subsequently grow more and more erotic, and will terminate in a certain expedited activity that my client has never attempted to deny, even if it's not an activity of the highest morality in the classical tradition, but rather in the erotic tradition. Even if his nearest and dearest were made to cruelly suffer from that unfortunate blunder. But bear in mind, ladies and gentlemen of the jury, that if there had been nobody in that hotel room that day, nothing would ever have happened, and today Jean-Jacques Hamilton would still have been counted among those who run the world.

JJH: (*Getting dressed and looking at his watch.*) You made me late, but it was worth it. What's your first name?

MARIAMA: Mariama.

JJH: I never pay for it, but I don't imagine you have an easy time of it in that jungle out there. (HE *slips several bills into her cleavage.*)

MARIAMA: (*Disappointed.*) Only $200?

JJH: Just a little present. (*Cynically.*) From my end, I never ask for anything. Not one red cent. (*Laughing.*) I'm a sexual philanthropist.

MARIAMA: (*Colder.*) You'll have to make it 1,000. You're rich.

JJH: I'm not Rockefeller. My job is to salvage all the others who were foolish enough to throw their money out the window.

HAMMOND: All that for exactly $800. That is the truth, the whole truth, and nothing but the truth. I ask you for the immediate release of my client and the complete and absolute restitution of his good name. Case dismissed, all the way down the line. It did not take place. It simply did not take place.

## SCENE FIFTEEN

JJH *is once again alone facing his interlocutor, but other characters* MARIAMA, MARIANNE, THE WHOMEVER *will burst on stage only to disappear around* HIM.

JJH: This is not a real pipe. The artist Magritte would have snickered. But you're not laughing. Me neither, when it comes right down to it. I live with a bad taste in my mouth. Hard to identify, a sort of human concentrate, a concentrate of all that is distinctly human. Not very edifying, if you see what I mean.

THE WHOMEVER: (*With a threatening look.*) You louse! With all that green you've got and your multiple underworld networks, you can pay off the judges and even the witnesses! Lousy asshole!

JJH: Everything seems to slip away in the end. There are times when I feel almost nothing at all, when I'm totally numb, even when it comes to dying. . . You could come tell me: "Hey there colon, you've got a nice little cancer of the colon," and I'd work to find a phrase that would earn me a place in the history books. Just to show up there even a tiny little bit.

THE WHOMEVER: (*Hysterical.*) The people love you! Don't give in! We've been behind you from the very first! We're all with you, JJH! JJH! JJH!

JJH: Am I going to be reduced to just three letters and nothing more? Who am I? I know less and less what the answer is, Doctor. How about you? Do you know who I am?

THE WHOMEVER: (*Bumping into* HIM *with a cell-phone.*) Hey! I could take a picture. Hey Superman! I friended you on Facebook!

MARIAMA: We're the only ones who know the truth.

JJH: But is it the same truth?

MARIAMA: You're the poison in my life.

JJH: The feeling's mutual.

MARIAMA: You're a real bastard.

JJH: Well, you're a real bitch.

MARIAMA: I no longer have a life.

JJH: Me neither, but you've become as famous as me. You could make a movie. Get a ghostwriter and write a book. (*Cynically.*) And your blowjobs are worth their weight in gold.

MARIAMA: I no longer have a life.

JJH: Life isn't worth all that much. It's death that's priceless. (*To his interlocutor.*) Not bad, hunh? (*To* MARIAMA.) Why don't we work out some kind of arrangement? It'd be less expensive. My wife'll pay just to get some peace.

THE WHOMEVER: (*Angrily.*) I don't give a damn about your fucking porn film. My factory's been shut down. Are you going to pay my debts or not?

JJH: Who am I, hunh? Who am I? Just an ordinary monster, same as you. As them? A man of power who did the best he could. An exceptional victim? (*Kidding.*) The Dreyfus of his age? Why don't you make up your mind? You'll never make up your mind. Your silences are pure gold. (*Short silence.*) Am I really free and clear? I'm nothing at all anymore. No further role to play. An empty stage. I what? Escaped from prison? But the looks people give me put me right back behind prison walls, shut me up behind bars that are a lot heavier. They make up fantasies about me. They don't look at me in the same way anymore. Hey look, the fucker's showing his face! Even you, even I see it!

THE WHOMEVER: Your wife, hats off! Wow! My old lady would never have believed it!

MARIANNE: My lady friends don't believe you. No one believes you.

JJH: You do. You believe me.

MARIANNE: I often have my doubts. But I prefer to believe you.

JJH: There was only one left. And you were it.

MARIANNE: You gave me the best and the worst.

JJH: Like anyone else would have done. The best and the worst.

MARIANNE: (*Coming over to* HIM.) I love you, simple as that.

JJH: (*Going over to* HER.) I was born with you, and I'll die with you.

THEY *hug, kiss.*

MARIANNE: Yes, I love you. But how long will it last?

JJH: (*Face to his interlocutor.*) The session will soon be over, Doctor. You always take a lot of notes right at the end. (*Short silence.*) This will be the last session. I never knew who I was. But even less who I wasn't. (HE *moves one of the chess pieces.*) Checkmate, Doctor! Checkmate! (*Short silence.* JJH *savors his victory.* HE *sends a text.*) I'll tell you what really happened that famous Thursday, at six minutes after noon in that hotel room number 7001, but. . . you'd never believe me.

**CURTAIN**

# THE SORCERERS

by

SERGE GORIELY

"Since the pioneering work of Cannon, we understand more clearly the psycho-physiological mechanisms underlying the instances reported from many parts of the world of death by exorcism and the casting of spells. An individual who is aware that he is the object of sorcery is thoroughly convinced that he is doomed according to the most solemn traditions of his group. His friends and relatives share this certainty. From then on the community withdraws. Standing aloof from the accursed, it treats him not only as though he were already dead, but as though he were a source of danger to the entire group. On every occasion and by every action, the social body suggests death to the unfortunate victim, who no longer hopes to escape what he considers to be his ineluctable fate. Shortly thereafter, sacred rites are held to dispatch him to the realm of shadows. First brutally torn from all of his family and social ties and excluded from all functions and activities through which he experienced self-awareness, then banished by the combined effect of intense terror, . . . and, finally, to the group's decisive reversal in proclaiming him—once a living man, with rights and obligations—dead and an object of fear, ritual, and taboo. Physical integrity cannot withstand the dissolution of the social personality."

Claude Lévi-Strauss, *Structural Anthropology*

## CAST

Luc

Paula

Chorus of Three Sorcerers

*The Chorus of Sorcerers may be played by a single actor as well as by several. One possible configuration, the one in this script, consists of a chorus of three, as follows:*

Sorcerer 1: An Elderly Lady, the Narrator of Yvonne's book, the Grandmother, and Nelson
Sorcerer 2: A Middle-Aged Woman, Luc's Mother, Nelson
Sorcerer 3: A Middle-Aged Man, Policeman, Luc's Father, and Nelson

*The scenes in which the Sorcerers are onstage should all be imbued with an atmosphere of unease and strangeness. They are not meant to be played realistically, but should rather suggest the interior lives of the protagonists. There is a lot of latitude for ways this ambience could be represented, but suffice to say that the scenes in question are denoted as "Mental Space."*

*When Paula speaks in her own Nigerian language, the English translation appears immediately after in brackets.*

## SCENE ONE
## "I'm Dreaming of a White Christmas"

LUC *and* PAULA *embracing—on a bench, on a sailing vessel, a room in a catering hall, no matter. Off to the side are discovered* SORCERERS 1, 2, *and* 3.

SORCERER 1: I think it's so nice
All love is nice
It's not whether you're white or black that counts but the fact that there's love
Yes the fact that there's love

SORCERER 2: Exactly
Love isn't about color

SORCERER 3: We can check back in a few months and see how it's going

SORCERER 1: Aaww, look at them

SORCERER 2: Ying and Yang

SORCERER 1: They're so cute

SORCERER 3: How times have changed

SOCERER 1: Ah, when I was young

SORCERER 3: Mixed marriages have become almost normal

SORCERER 2: What country is she from actually?

SORCERER 1: May your days be merry and bright (*Softly singing a song like* "I'm Dreaming of a White Christmas.")

SORCERER 2: Maybe she's running away from some war

SORCERER 3: When one white's with another it's no bed of roses either

SORCERER 2: In bed with his mother?

SORCERER 3: No, I said two whites in bed with each other

SORCERER 1: (*Singing song low.*) . . .With every Christmas card I write. . .

SORCERER 3: If you like getting involved in political causes
Thanks just the same, I'm fine with the whole thing

SORCERER 1: (*Still singing.*) And may all your Christmases be white

SORCERER 2: Who knows it might last

SORCERER 3: Make the most the most of it while you're still young

SORCERER 2: I devoutly wish that they do
And that it enriches both their lives

SORCERER 1: Always love each other always

SORCERER 2: I don't think they can hear us from where we're standing

SORCERER 3: I don't mind African music

SORCERER 1: Good for you
Love each other until death do you part

SORCERER 2: Yes, we should give them encouragement
Good for you

SORCERER 3: But I have a little trouble pronouncing those names
Miriam Makeeper

SORCERER 2: So do I
I really like jazz a lot

SORCERER 1: Go ahead you say something nice to them too

SORCERER 2: Go ahead
It'll make them feel good

SORCERER 3: Please, let's not be so juvenile
Don't treat me like a child

SORCERER 2: (*To 3.*) In the future all we'll see is mixing of the races

SORCERER 3: That's what I hear

SORCERER 2: We wish you every happiness in the world

SORCERER 3: Nothing can stand in the way of my happiness for them

SORCERER 2: That's nice

SORCERER 3: If it works out

SORCERER 1: Love will find a way

SORCERER 2: May it last forever

SORCERER 3: You'll need all the courage you can muster

## SCENE TWO
## "The Love Nest"

*In the Apartment.*

LUC *and* SORCERER 3, *in the character of a* POLICEMAN.

LUC: (*Nervous, seemingly upbeat.*) Come in make yourself at home
Come in
That's where she sat yes in the middle
The apartment not the same anymore
You lit it up Paula
You were the light
Not bad
Not a palace but it was here waiting for you waiting for us
It was all we had but that was all we needed
You and me here
Here love nest
Lo-ove
A nest in which you were my light

The silence how many times, my African Queen
A look sufficed
Miracle just
Only the need to
Eyes you in mine me swimming around so small in yours
You who understood me so well yes so well
Yes you the third eye the sixth sense
Simply savoring the moment

How many times time stopped
Before in each others' arms flesh against flesh

*At the Immigration Office.*

SORCERER 3: (*In a rage, with a marked tough policeman's voice.*) As far as I'm concerned that's not her not her in the photo
They can't get into our country so easy mister
And you think a letter of invitation's all it takes
But when it comes down to it all the same
A little bird tells me she didn't come here to work

LUC: To save yourself they said
From who from me

SORCERER 3: You never know
I don't see nothing stamped on your forehead
To prove you're not just some pimp

LUC: Stupid assholes
This fist
See this fist
I don't know what got into me but their sickening kissers
Human pieces of shit
They deserved it

SORCERER 3: I'm sorry I'll have to send her back that's the law
Hey what's wrong with you
Stay right where you are I'm telling you this room is off limits
Ouch ouch ouch arrest that nutcase

LUC: Trained to corner attack like a Doberman fuck them up
Put an end to their lousy lives
Like pit bulls killer dogs
To kill they're born like that mean
There are people like that mean to the bone like that
But it's the system makes them that way
Gets them worked up so's they'll bite wound grind to a powder people like you who
I know I shouldn't have they've got the upper hand
The border
My fists were how you got through it
But the others
People like you who

SORCERER 3: Boy he can hit the bastard
Go ahead Joey show him
What the fuck is he doing
Go ahead guys give Joey a hand go ahead

LUC: No it doesn't hurt it'll pass
Oh if I'd only been able to
Get a hold of their ugly kissers and bash 'em to pieces
One of them sure as hell knows I landed him one you can bet your life

SORCERER 3: Heh heh calm down guys not too hard
Heh heh don't actually smash his head
Get him into handcuffs
Oh you wanted to see your Juliet, Romeo
Last name first name address
You'll get your chocolate bar back later

LUC: My love you having to deal with those mangy dogs those racist cops those Gestapo bastards
The whole lot of us just a bunch of hypocrites always saying we live in a democracy
We're so naive bragging about standing up for civil liberties
To the outside world sure to the outside world
But it'll have to start on our own doorstep
The whole lot of us holier-than-thou put your own house in order
O.T.V.T.
I scared them off decided it's better to bide my time
Otherwise you'd be on an airplane right now gagged handcuffed tied down
O.T.V.T. Order to vacate the territory
Prohibited from living together
So far away Nigeria
How could we ever have

SORCERER 3: One more guy stung by the African Fly
Pull yourself together guy forget her
Take my word for it
It wouldn't work anyhow

LUC: A world of barbarians
Every social grouping has to have a father in it
If there's no father you're screwed devoid of value
A father with all his pals all his contacts his lawyers

It's like in Nigeria the strength of the tribe without it you're screwed
Render unto Caesar what is Caesar's
If not for my father's lawyer the great De Wolf we'd've been screwed

*The Holding Cell.*

SORCERER 3: Hey wake up it's morning
Just got a call
There out you go
Fuck me I don't get it but you're some lucky bastard
Take it from an experienced cop if anyone deserved to go to trial you did
Out you go get moving the two of you I said

LUC: Damn straight we were lucky
But it's an outrage to have to rely on dumb luck
Relying on dumb luck
Whatever happened to human justice
Luck's all that matters
Being born a Belgian citizen to a daddy who had the same dumb luck

SORCERER 3: One little piece of advice
They've got their eye on you
You've got a sham marriage
If she doesn't see the lead in your pencil we'll nab your sweetheart
Before you can turn around
If it wasn't me, somebody else would
Better believe it and next time for good
Straight to the detention center she'll go
I'll tell you a good one you listen to me
Lock-up yeah house of little or no repute hah hah
You no capeesh repute hah hah jail

LUC: Hah hah Belgians are so refined such great conversationalists
I'll tell you a good one the fight goes on
Hope's all very well but we need to be prepared to flex our muscles
That's not all there is to Belgium
Belgium is also my father my mother my friends their friends
All ready to fight
Fight for real values
Equality justice and democracy
Belgium can be a perfectly good place to live
You'll see I guarantee you a good place to live
Like right here this love nest
A good place to live and be happy

## SCENE THREE
## "They!"

*In the Apartment.*

PAULA *is in a feverish state.* LUC *is discomfited.*

LUC: Yes, I understand.

PAULA: *Na san yadda na ji.* [I know how I feel] It's not what I eat. I know my body.

LUC: *(Without having understood.)* It's the nourishment. What you eat.

PAULA: *Ya yi wani abu.* [It's something else] . . . I've traveled before. Never any problem, never with the food. *Yake ciwo* [It hurts]. *Ashe, ba ku gane ba? A tuburkumara.* [Don't you understand? Not my stomach.] *Duk jikina cutar.* [My whole body hurts.] Not my stomach. My whole body hurts. My arms, my neck, my legs. . . *Dukan jiki* [The whole body] I don't eat with my legs!

LUC: It can go on like that for years! I'll say it again. It is now November. Six months! Six months isn't long enough. Your body's going to need time to get used to things. I'm telling you. It's not only the food, it's the air, the cold, it's November, the germs. . . It's all been scientifically proven! It'll just have to take time. And going to the doctor is important, the doctor's important.

PAULA: You, you don't believe. You, you don't believe in anything. But I, yes, I do believe.

LUC: Well I believe in reason!

PAULA: It's them! *Su, su, su.* [Them, them, them.] *Kowa ba ne* [No more].

LUC: And reason tells me to believe in a psychosomatic connection!

PAULA: *Babu! Babu ! Babu!* [No! No! No!] I'm not going to see your Raymond. Never again.

LUC: (*To himself.*) Everything's against me! That's it! The whole world against me.

PAULA: Your friend!

LUC: Even so. He could help you. He's a doctor, my friend.

PAULA: Not Raymond. Not him. No doctor. No.

LUC: And anyway it isn't true. I'm not saying there's no supernatural factor here. I believe in the supernatural. All I'm saying is we should take it one step at a time. Mustn't rush things. And consider supernatural causes afterwards. After ruling out all the other hypotheses.

PAULA: (*In pain again.*) *Wan!* [Ow!]

LUC: If you'd at least take some anti-pain medication. Good medicine. Anti-pain. Good medicine. Take it, I'm telling you.

PAULA: *Su!* [Them!] Them are too close.

LUC: (*Correcting.*) THEY are too close.

PAULA: How them're looking at me!

LUC: (*Losing his temper.*) Them, them them! Always them!

PAULA: *Amininki sharri ne* [Your friend is bad]. Raymond is bad. You went to school with him? Nothing doing. He's bad. He looks at me. He touches me. Everything I have inside me. Inside. He's bad. *Bacin tunani* [Evil mind]. Not because he's a doctor! You don't understand. *Ba don likita ne. Haba! Don me ba kwa gane*? [Not because he's a doctor. Oh no! Why don't you understand?]

LUC: Good bad. Black white. There's a lot more to life than you might imagine.

PAULA: There is something in their mind, something wrong, don't you understand? They want, they want me. . .

LUC: Want what? If my father takes your hands. . .

PAULA: Very hard, he squeezes. . . it's not normal! He squeezes my body, gives me kisses all over. . . Ah! I feel bad!

LUC: Excess of affection!

PAULA: When your mother smiles, I see she wants to eat! Yes, I see it. She wants to eat me, me! Your mother! I'm not her daughter! She can't say I'm her daughter!

LUC: (*To himself, imitating* PAULA.) Always show respect for older people, Luc. And especially towards parents! They gave you life. You have to learn how to forgive. . .

PAULA: What?

LUC: Nothing! I'd better not say any more.

PAULA: Say! Talk! You're hiding. Speak.

LUC: You're extreme, too extreme!

PAULA: What?

LUC: My mother, a retired English teacher, turning into a harpy, an old cannibalistic sorcerer? My father, how do you see him? A rapist! And my best friend someone who casts spells, and lusts after you to boot? That's what I mean by extreme! Your point of view is too extreme. How do you want me to speak? I can't tell you anything! Talking to you's impossible!

PAULA *has more intense pain in her belly.*

PAULA: *Wan! Wan!*

LUC: Paula?

PAULA: You don't feel anything? You don't feel anything in your body? It's against you too! I know you! If you're suffering it's because of them! *Yama! Yama!* [Help!]

LUC: Is something wrong?

PAULA: *Yama! Yama!* Brother!

LUC: This time, I'm taking you to see Raymond! It might not be the digestion, but one thing's for sure, it is the nerves. . .

PAULA: *Ba a taba ni.* [Don't touch me!] I'm not crazy!

LUC: Even so, you're hallucinating about your brother. . .

PAULA: I'm not crazy!

LUC: No, you're suffering. . . It's not madness, but suffering. . . So, get dressed and. . .

*Silence.* PAULA *puts distance between herself and* LUC.

PAULA: My parents didn't understand, I know, they didn't understand, my brother is dead. I knew about the two businessmen. I knew who they were. I still know now. I know. Who listens to a little girl? I was very little. Parents don't listen to little girls. *"Rufe!"* ["Shut up!"] They believed my brother. My brother is big, the biggest of all my brothers. "Shut up, shut up!" I'm not a little girl anymore. "Shut up, shut up!" Luc, you hear me? My brother went to Lagos with them. And with all the money. They ate a lot. My mother's a very good cook. You want me to eat too? You want me to eat like my brother? My brother died after! I yell, yell: "Don't go! Brother, don't go!" No one listens. You don't listen either. I know that he's not coming back and for days on end he doesn't come back. I hear him: "Paula, Paula! *Yama! Yama!* Help me!" He's lying there under the house. I know. His arms, his back, his mouth. The blood's coming out. He has his body under the house, in the earth. *"Yama, yama, yama!"* I'm there with ropes tied around my bed. I have fever. It hurts. My parents think: Paula is crazy! I yell, *"Tafi gidan."* ["Go to the house."] "Go quickly, the house, go to the house, my brother is dying, I see him. *Tafi gidan!"* No one does something. They think I'm crazy and that everything's alright. My mother gives me water. But I see it: My brother's dying. And later, my parents see I'm right. . .

*Silence.*

You think I'm crazy, Luc? I see him under the house. . . He yells I yell. For days, days, days, he yells, lying there under the house. I yell, I'm not crazy. I have a lot of fever. *Ruwa! Ruwa!* [water!] White spots appear, white circles, larger. Water! I can't breathe. . .

LUC, *beside himself, wants to comfort her.*

LUC: Paula, get a grip on yourself! Paula, you want some water? Paula, I'm with you.

## SCENE FOUR
## "Hello Mom"

*Mental Space.*

LUC *studies the cell-phone.* SORCERER 2 *(acting the role of* LUC'S MOTHER*) is behind him.*

SORCERER 2: The whole month, hunh?
I see, you're going to be busy all month, is that right
What are you talking about I never heard of any such agency
Oh so they might be interested photos of Africa hunh
At least your trip to Paris won't have been a total waste
I wouldn't be so sure
You haven't got anything in writing

LUC: I see, nothing I do is any good.
Thank you

SORCERER 2: Well I think you're trying to avoid us
How can you say such a thing or even think it
I respect you
Enormously
You're my son my only son my very-own-Luc
If I lose you I lose everything
We never see each other as it is
Never I'm telling you
But I'm not dramatizing
Call it dramatizing if you like but that's what I feel inside
I'm your mother I carried you in my womb I fed brushed diapered

LUC: Punished shut up yelled hit tortured ruined for life

SORCERER 2: Luc you've changed and I'm not the only one who's noticed
Papa is very very very unhappy
Yes of course I'm listening to you
We her new family
Funny hunh
Ah ah ah
She doesn't even attend classes anymore
And without a decent knowledge of French
Oh you may say there are jobs where she wouldn't need French
But you know what that means
You know why you don't need French there

That's what you want
Her new family's a lie
Besides she hates my cooking
No surprise there

LUC: In light of the way you cook

SORCERER 2: In light of where she comes from
But it's worse if she doesn't say anything
Because I see it I can feel it
Oh I'm not some cake-baking grandma you can just roll around in her own dough
Oh oh oh go ahead and laugh
We'll see who laughs last
I know the two of you make fun of me
You're telling me she loved that stew I made
That stew was a flop
Yes yes I know when they turn out bad

LUC: You're the only one who thinks so

SORCERER 2: No no I don't buy it—she's not as shy as all that no no
I say it's high time she made some effort
Me for example

LUC: Her for example

SORCERER 2: Oh it wasn't so simple at the beginning with your grandmother either you know
Your Nonny
But I made an effort a major effort
Result being our relationship is now perfect

LUC: Hypocrite

SORCERER 2: That's the only way to say it perfect
I always say that learn that life the best teacher
You never get everything you want right away
You've got to be ready to ap-ply your-self.

LUC: Hello Mom
Your son is happy because he loves
Help him understand him

SORCERER 2: You ask me to imagine what
Oh but your father is Belgian I'm sorry
I don't see why I have to imagine him as a black man
I'm perfectly content with your papa
Who is white and Belgian

LUC: (*Laughing.*) Belgian waffles, Belgian Red Devils, Belgian pure white chocolate.

SORCERER 2: Aaaaaaah if I were Belgian and him African
And living in Africa to boot
Well I would have been interested in their customs
I would have tried to make myself useful
I would have learned their language
Really applying myself not one day on one day off
Oh I'm sorry what does she do all day long anyway
She reads
What type of books
But she tidies up and cleans in any case
Sleeps the whole time, does she?

LUC: If you only knew Mom

SORCERER 2: What vomiting and stomach cramps
Oh my God maybe it's serious
Why didn't you say anything

LUC: Hmm, I wonder why I didn't

SORCERER 2: Well I get worried when there's a good reason to worry

LUC: The truth is I don't trust

SORCERER 2: And she has a temperature
Weird

LUC: Weird weird she said weird

SORCERER 2: But she's got to eat
Oh she's absolutely got to eat
There are so many sicknesses out there you never know
And she comes from Africa to boot

LUC: To boot

SORCERER 2: But you my dear of course I'm your mother I worry about you
You be careful
And of everything
Understand
Of everything

LUC: And you you understand me

SORCERER 2: And what did Raymond say
Can't see you for ten days
Oh please this isn't a joking matter
And to think that he's your friend
You considered going to the emergency room
I'll stop by tomorrow
Oranges
She must like oranges
Or better yet bananas
She prefers bananas no

LUC: AAA-UNHUNHUNH-AAAH! (*The Johnny Weissmuller yell.*) Long live Tarzan

SORCERER 2: Of course I don't mind of course not
I'm your mother and I love Paula a great deal
Just tell me when
I'm your mother and we're supposed to face up to adversity no
Luc Luc
Hello hello

## SCENE FIVE
## "Flowers"

*In the apartment,* LUC, *a bouquet of flowers in his hand, is talking to* PAULA.

LUC: It's definite. You're pregnant.

PAULA: Definite.

LUC: Raymond is positive.

PAULA: Ah!

LUC: I was sure that's what it was! You were too. How could we have been so clueless! You feel better now?

*Silence.*

PAULA: And what do you want to do?

LUC: What I want to do?

PAULA: Yes.

LUC: The way you see it? What are these flowers for?

PAULA: So, there won't be an. . .

LUC: Unless you've changed your mind. . .

PAULA: Me?

LUC: Right?

PAULA: Luc!

LUC: So we won't do anything.

*Silence.*

LUC: We've got to strike while the iron is hot. This news will help us to forge ahead. . . Our meeting each other was Phase 1, marriage was Phase 2, the baby will be Phase 3. . . We bow before a new dimension to. . .

PAULA: (*Humming low in Nigerian.*) Djina-a-a. . .

LUC: It may be tough going. It's unquestionably going to be tough, but I just know I'll rise to the occasion. I'm ready, willing, and able. . . and I'll redouble my efforts. . .

PAULA: Djina-a-a. . .

LUC: Already talking to it, hunh?

PAULA: I feel it.

LUC: Really?

PAULA: Yes.

LUC: Not a little too early? Raymond told me that. . . are you listening to me? Hey! Hey! It's going to be the 22nd . . . 22nd of August.

PAULA: (*Distracted, massaging her belly.*) Ah! August.

LUC: August 22nd. You're in your fifth week. Fifth! We just put our heads together and figured it out.

PAULA: Ah!

LUC: He made me a list of everything you can and can't eat. He says that the test results are excellent. He's rarely seen a body in such good condition. You'll have to go back and see him again. I made an appointment for next week.

PAULA: I feel it, I feel it.

LUC: May I touch too?

PAULA: You won't hurt him?

LUC: Me?

PAULA: (*Letting him touch.*) Life is sacred.

LUC: Hurt it! I may have my faults, but when I give my word it means something. I was following a different train of thought. . . I was talking in the abstract, you know? General principles! Even if he's smaller than a peanut, it's my child! How could you imagine that I'd harm a hair of his head. . . ? The little peanut?

PAULA: Luc. . . You're fabulous!

LUC: It's our child, Paula. Our child. (*With a gesture of mutual tenderness.*)

PAULA: I want to go back to class.

LUC: Well what do you know!

PAULA: (*Rubbing her belly.*) I can do a lot of things with him. I want to graduate. Now especially. I think I'll have to re-register.

LUC: Wait. I think, I'm only expressing one point of view, and of course I may be wrong. . . It's my impression that you've never really felt a strong desire or need to study. You know what I mean? That you never really wanted to.

PAULA: What!?

LUC: It's not a criticism. . . I think it was my fault. My fault entirely. I put ideas into your head which are based on my desires and wishes, not yours. I'm done with that. It's not surprising that you gave it up. But I don't blame you. Not in the least.

PAULA: I want to study.

LUC: You're acting as if I was trying to deprive you of something, but it's not like that. I only think that this isn't the right moment for you to be going to school. Anybody can take classes, but it's stupid to do it if you feel like someone's forcing you to, even your own husband. On the other hand, later on if it turns out that you simply must get a degree and you believed deep down that you'd go back and sign up right away, no problem, money's no object. . . And you can study exactly what you feel like studying, I swear! Yes, yes, I insist. . . Cooking or hairdressing are every bit as good as law or medicine. No one would think otherwise. I'm not hell-bent on your getting a G.E.D. I don't give a damn what anyone else thinks. I want you to feel free! The main thing is for a person to do what they want and to do it well!

*Silence.*

PAULA: I want to speak French well.

LUC: Your French is wonderful. There's no need for you to take any more classes in it. You could keep studying English with my mother. You've made terrific progress. You're already there. . . Go out there and knock 'em dead!

PAULA: Kill them?

LUC: You're as prepared as any soldier! Maybe not a general, meaning a French teacher, but any other rank, you're up there with the best of 'em. There's no question. Any recruiter in Belgium would hire you, I'm absolutely sure. You'd get the job. You understand? Belgium wants you! You have nothing to worry about! But (*Tapping her belly.*) first you've got another battle to fight right here.

## SCENE SIX
## "The Future Lion"

*In the Apartment.*

PAULA *is six months pregnant.* SORCERER 2 *(in the character of* THE MOTHER*) is behind her.*

PAULA: Listen my Nelson
I needed to eat
I needed you to eat
I needed to ate
I needed to have aten
I needed all of us to have aten
I needed I needed

SORCERER 2: Fine that's just fine to start with
Continue

PAULA: You'll speak my Nelson
You'll speak better than me
You won't laugh at me hm
You shouldn't laugh at other people and never at parents
You won't be bad you'll never be bad
You'll be my honey my lion my sun
Don't be afraid my Nelson
The house will be your castle

SORCERER 2: I warn you English is not an easy language

PAULA: Ca-stle the tee is silent
Only good people will be accepted except good people
We only accept good people
Except accept

Accept except
In the street expect no cars nothing except birds
Expect accept except

SORCERER 2: Oh yes I'm sure
Who wouldn't like The Little Prince
And later you could read Catcher in the Rye and even Macbeth

PAULA: No only birds
And the sky the sky too and the stars in the dark the stars
Candles of life in the night
Can-dles-of-life

SORCERER 2: What do you say we do a little geography now

PAULA: I saw your bed all the toys your desk
Your papa wants you to have a desk
Papa loves you a lot
You'll be a good student and he'll be proud of you
You can feel it when I touch you yes you feel it
Ma-ma ma-ma
No no don't be impatient wait the house will come
One day Papa will be rich from his photos
We have to wait and be diplomatic

SORCERER 2: Belgium is divided into three regions three
Flanders Wallonia and don't forget Brussels

PAULA: Di-plo-ma-tic
Everyone serves a purpose even bad people
Nice with them nice with us you have to understand why
There are less marriages because of winter
Belgians don't get married when it's cold out
The less photos the less money you understand Paula
And as for reporting
Because of the economic crisis the agencies don't want to buy articles
Your mommy likes to show herself off
Dress up pretty
Not good we've got to cut corners
Hey mister lion it's too soon for you to come out
I said wait
Fine

SORCERER 2: Yes yes Brussels is also a region

PAULA: I had to be your mama
You had to be my son
You had to be
No not my pal
Your bed Papa's bed
It had to be us

SORCERER 2: The Signal of Botrange 759 yards high the highest point in Belgium
Paula are you listening to me
In Nigeria the mountains are higher I suppose

PAULA: Where you war
War you were
We where happy
There certainly war two men
Two happy men

SORCERER 2: Good stop that's enough for today

PAULA: War you where brought into the world to war
Papa's clothes
Papa-baby

SORCERER 2: For Monday I propose we dive right into chapter five

PAULA: His mother kept everything for you
And the baby carriage and the toys too
They're very rich and want to help us
They have the same blood
You have to respect them
They love you
I don't care one way or the other

SORCERER 2: And have a look at pages 26 27 and 83 that'll do

PAULA: They are your grandparents
Don't be afraid Nelson
Everything will be fine
Your Papa thinks about you a lot.

## SCENE SEVEN
## "At the Hospital"

*In the Maternity Ward.*

PAULA *is lying down, her baby in her arms.* SHE *finishes nursing, lays it down by her side.* LUC *enters, dirty, with a backpack.*

LUC: It's me! Show him to me. Where is the little tike? (*To the baby.*) You couldn't wait, you little scamp. One shove and bloop. Like a letter in the mailbox. How smooth his skin is! It looks like a veil stretched over the bones. (*To* PAULA.) Please excuse the accoutrement. (*To the baby.*) Ah, my very own little flea, I could eat you up. . . (*Kissing* PAULA.) I'm totally beat.

PAULA: I wasn't able to call you.

LUC: If you only knew! It's absolutely untenable! They wanted blood and gore. They wanted a horror show. Well, they'll get what they asked for!

*Silence.*

PAULA: She didn't want me to make phone calls.

LUC: Who? No!

PAULA: Yes!

LUC: Ah! Right, the deposit for the phone. She mentioned that.

PAULA: I couldn't tell you about the birth of your son before your mother?

LUC: That's too bad, I know.

PAULA: She said the phone didn't work!

LUC: If you want me to I'll talk to her.

PAULA: I hate her!

LUC: Calm down! It's a big day!

PAULA: You'll talk to her? Like hell you will! You're not even pissed off!

LUC: Yes, yes, I am pissed off, very pissed off.

*Silence.*

PAULA: She could call you whenever she wanted! Anyone could call you, but me, your wife, no!

LUC: (*Caressing the baby.*) I called you three times. Three!

PAULA: Don't wake Nelson!

LUC (*Pulling back.*) My hands are clean! I was in the heart of the jungle.

PAULA: And here I was all alone! To watch me give birth, that she wanted, but to let me make a phone call, no!

*Silence.*

LUC (*Bored.*) Paula... By the way...

PAULA: What!

LUC: Parents are parents and as far as they're concerned, I'm thinking about my father in particular, it's very important that... You know, respect your elders...

PAULA: You promised!

LUC: Promised, no. I must have said, "Doubtless," "most likely," "almost promised," but promised-promised, no. In any case, I promised them, promised-promised... Them. I can't turn back the clock even if I wanted to. And anyway, Nelson's the name of a military hero and I don't like anything having to do with the military.

PAULA: You don't like kings either.

LUC: I had to choose. And between the two, the one Belgian, the other English... It's a name that's resilient, full-bodied, like a fine wine that's had a chance to age.

PAULA: (*Serious.*) My son isn't wine! (*Laugh.*) Albert!?

LUC: Oh! Why does it have to be so hard? There I was, I was standing... in front of a hundred fifty three corpses. A hundred fifty three! These guys had been thrown into cages. Horrendous agony. Drowned, all of them! And at that very moment, my father there on the telephone. You understand? Albert simply came to be beyond question. The name of the father my father's father. To give some sense to what I was seeing. That's why.

*Silence.*

PAULA: The child was coming and you knew it. You wanted to go away instead and why? To see dead people?

LUC: I didn't want to. It's my job. We'd talked it over. An incredible opportunity.

PAULA: You want to see me lying in a coffin?

LUC: What are you talking about? I love you. Ah! Let's get down to the matter at hand. Look at the little animal! (LUC *takes a camera out of his knapsack, holds it out to* PAULA *who is indifferent.*) It's called a Leica. Look at these lenses, this viewfinder. . . Here, take it. Pretty impressive, hm? The best camera in the world. Without that I could never have gone to the Philippines. I absolutely had to have a Leica. 5,000 Euros.

PAULA: So?

LUC: My parents loaned me the money. I can pay them back whenever I want. I'm in debt.

PAULA: Give them back the money.

LUC: The camera's been bought.

PAULA: Return the camera.

LUC: That's not how it works. . . A deal's a deal. Besides, they gave me double that.

PAULA: Ten thousand

LUC: The hospital, pampers, it all adds up. But. . . I had an idea. . . we could sublet. . . Marion and Loic would be interested. . .

PAULA: What about us?

LUC: There's the studio.

PAULA: I won't go!

LUC: 400 a month! 400. That's how we make ends meet! My parents wouldn't make us pay a cent!

PAULA: Wait. I don't understand. They lose money, and then. . . They want to help us, ask them for money. They give you 10,000 Euros, and we stay in our home! That I'd agree to.

LUC: You make everything more complicated!

PAULA: I know them. They don't know how to give. You whites don't know how to give! Always thinking how to win out over others. You talk, you talk a lot, but you lie. They only want us to go live in their place. Only they never mention that it isn't their place at all! The studio apartment's in the same building! So you still want to go live in their place? They want to pull the wool over your eyes. . . to take us and everything we've got. Take Nelson. That's what you want, isn't it? No, no, never! Are you like them? Luc are you just like them?

## SCENE EIGHT
## "1,2, 3 and 4"

*In the Apartment.*

LUC *and* PAULA *with their baby.* LUC *dressed in African garb, is slightly drunk.* HE *is dancing to African instrumental music.* PAULA *moves along with* HIM, *a book in her hand.*

LUC: (*Throwing himself into dancing and singing to the music.*) Wowoowowowow (*To* PAULA.) I'm getting the hang of it, I'm getting the hang of it.

PAULA: (*Setting the rhythm.*) 1-2-3 and 4. . . 1-2-3 and 4.

LUC: Keep going! Next sentence!

PAULA: (*Reading.*) "The earth offers you up its riches and you shall not want for anything. . ."

LUC: Sun. Shade. Animals. Fruits. Dream with us Albert.

PAULA: (*Reading.*) "You will want for nothing. . ."

LUC: And cool cool cool beer all you can drink in the dry dry dry brush shesh shesh. Wowoowowowo.

PAULA: ". . .on condition that you know how to open your hands"

LUC: Yes, absolutely open your hands and have lots and lots piles of friends, friends. "Fill up my glass, my friend!" Wowoowowow "One more and I drink"

PAULA: Keep going?

LUC: Of course. It gets things moving, doesn't it? "One more and I'm off." Wowoowowow. Am I alright?

PAULA: You're alright. (*Reading.*) "You shall be together in the silent memory of God. . ."

LUC: God! God! (*Toasting God.*) Cheers!

PAULA: "When the white wings of death scatter your days"

LUC: Everybody! Chip chip chip! Death! (*Keeping to the rhythm.*) Keep going! Next!

PAULA *leafs through the book.* LUC *impatient.*

LUC: You can't find it!? Give me that book. (*He takes* PAULA*'s book, leafs through it*). Ah! Here it is! (*Reading.*) "the children and the sons and the daughters. . ." (*To* ALBERT.) Are you listening, Albert? This concerns you.

PAULA: Your feet, Luc. They've lost the rhythm.

LUC: ". . . are the sons and the daughters of love of life itself." Wowoowowow. Life for its own sake, Paula. (*To* ALBERT.) And then you'll be a man my son.

PAULA: Look at your feet.

LUC: Paula, I'm having an epiphany.

PAULA: (*Laughing at* LUC, *who loses the beat.*) Oh, Luc, what are you doing?

LUC: (*Half-joking, half serious.*) It's no use trying to change the world and no good badmouthing the stupidity of people.

PAULA: You're worse than an elephant!

LUC: Listen! Each person's got to change themselves. Find out how to live, to be happy, get his own soul to grow, make it beautiful.

PAULA: Be quiet and look!

LUC: Hunh?

PAULA: You've lost the beat completely.

LUC: That's all there is to life! To become a better person!

PAULA: You have to concentrate! That's not what we call dancing in Africa.

LUC: No?

PAULA: No! (*Showing* HIM.) Look: 1-2-3 and 4. . .1-2-3 and 4. Okay, now you do it

LUC: 1-2, 1-2, 1-2. No! 1-2-3 and 4. It's not that hard. 1-2-3 and 4. Like that?

PAULA: 1-2-3 and 4, 1-2-3 and 4.

LUC: (*Picking it up.*) Me, an elephant. . . ? I'm an elephant?

PAULA: Dance! 1-2-3 and 4. . .1-2-3 and 4.

LUC: (*Mixing a tune from "The Lion King" with the music that's playing.)* "Our little Albert, what a wonderful phrase . . ."

PAULA: 1-2-3 and 4, 1-2-3 and 4

LUC: All together. "Our little Albert ain't no passing craze. . ."

PAULA: Be quiet. 1-2-3 and 4. 1-2-3 and 4.

LUC: "Our little Albert ain't no passing craze."

PAULA: 1-2-3 and 4. 1-2-3 and 4.

## SCENE NINE
## "Yvonne's Book"

*In the Apartment.*

PAULA, *on the telephone.* SORCERER 1 *(Relaying the ideas from* YVONNE.*) is in front of* HER.

PAULA: Yesterday the dragon went out of the house.

SORCERER 1: Rouah-rouah-rouah

PAULA: He wasn't very pleased
It's on account of me
I'm not strong enough
I doubt him
That's not good
He shouted spit flames
Stop crying it's for the money we have no choice
So then I asked him to forgive me
I don't want to live in a rat-hole either
Mama Mama what was it like with Papa
Maybe Luc doesn't like my body anymore
Men don't like women who've had babies
And yet I let him do anything
Anything
Anything
Maybe he wants things I don't know
Mama the pain's come back
I just grit my teeth
It wasn't because of Nelson after all
That morning I vomited
I think I'm a *bangawa*
But nobody can help me
Yvonne gave me an address
But Luc won't let me go
He thinks they're quacks thieves
You were sad when I left the village
You told me that Luc was good
Yes he's good
The woman has to see the man as better than he is and that way he'll become so
That's what Yvonne's book says

SORCERER 1: I admire him I approve of him I encourage him I trust him I accept him
Repeat

PAULA: I admire him I approve of him I encourage him I trust him I accept him

SORCERER 1: Repeat

PAULA: I admire him I approve of him I encourage him

## SCENE TEN
## "The Argument"

*In the Apartment.*

PAULA *discovered. Enter* LUC.

LUC: Nelson sleeping?

PAULA: Yes.

LUC: He's sleeping? That's good.

PAULA: . . .

LUC: Paula. . .

*Silence.*

LUC: Yesterday, I met Beatrice.

PAULA: Ah!

LUC: She ran after me. I didn't want to talk to her. No! Talk to her. . .no! She insisted and. . . I found out certain things. . . rumors! Yes, rumors!

PAULA: Why do you listen to it?

LUC: What she says confirms what I've already been suspecting. She's totally bent out of shape about it. She's in our court. She likes us. So why shouldn't I listen to her?

*Silence.*

LUC: You know what people are saying about you, meaning, about us? Not her. Unh unh. She, she's only reporting what they say. She, she's furious, I'm telling you. She's on our side. Those people, the others, my "friends," so-called friends. You know what they're saying, hm?

PAULA: That I'm black.

LUC: That you shut yourself up in the house, that you don't want anyone to get a glimpse of Nelson, and least of all your in-laws. . . they're saying. That's what they're saying.

PAULA: Oh!

LUC: That you're selfish, that you're bad for me. They say that too.

PAULA: And do you think I'm bad for you?

LUC: You hear the kinds of things they think they have every right to say! And that they don't have the courage to say to your face. Cowards, a bunch of lousy gossips! It all slips by under the radar. As for taking responsibility for their actions: Zero! It's all done by adding little touches, details that gradually mount up. What a world! My world, don't you know! No one claims responsibility, but a self-multiplying monster is taking shape.

PAULA: I just asked you—if I'm bad for you? Am I bad for you or not?

LUC: Of course not! But we have to talk about it, don't we? We have to talk about it! What am I supposed to make of all these criticisms I'm hearing? I ask you, what am I supposed to do with them?

PAULA: It's not you, Luc. It's not you.

LUC: It's become unlivable for me here! Yes, unlivable! And I'm not talking about biological life. I mean the life of the mind. The mind, what goes on in the heart, in the head. Stop seeing them? Refuse to listen to them? Just like that? (HE *claps his hands.*) All over, just like that. (HE *claps again.*) A clap of the hands and it ceases to exist! What a sensational magic trick that would be, wouldn't it? You retreat into your cave, wrap yourself in your cocoon up to the gills, and they cease to exist! But what happens the next day? And the day after? Hunh? And the one that comes after the day after that, when you want to come out of hibernation? 'Cause these four walls are suffocating, a prison covered with peeling colored wallpaper, with pipes sticking through, with a stinking carpet. No, it's actually a cage in the zoo! 'Cause they all know what's going on in here and they're licking their chops over it. It's gotten so bad that I'm scared I'll run into someone I know when I go out. 'Sgotten to the point that I hug the walls like an illegal immigrant, endure the stares from every native Belgian I bump into! It's easy to say you shouldn't care, that they're all just a bunch of envious losers without a scrap of dignity in their hearts, unworthy and lacking the courage we have. It's too easy! You can't turn your back on your whole family, everyone you know, and all your fellow countrymen in one fell swoop! You may say that that's just what you did. But it's not the same thing. You didn't grow up here. I have a whole life behind me here. The streets, the parks, the smells, the faces. Most important the faces. I know them all. I'm a constituent part of this city whether I want to be or not. I'm a part of it. I realize now that I've committed a major transgression. I wanted to overturn the order of things. A madman! I'm the drop of water who said to the ocean—I've had it with being salty!

*Silence.*

LUC: (*Grimacing.*) Bulubululu! I said bulubululu! No reaction? Bulubulubulu? Don't care to laugh?

PAULA *gets up and starts to make for the exit.*

LUC: We need to protect ourselves from spell-throwers, don't we? Can't become *bangawas*, can we? Bulululu! Bulubulu! Paula, can't you summon up a little sense of humor? That's how they see us! Paula, I'm trying to be make you laugh. A smidgeon of good manners in the midst of our despair, for the love of God! Stay, stay here, I'm telling you. . .

*Silence.* PAULA *sits back down.*

LUC: And if, and if. . . And what if. . . It's a question, right? What if there were still overtures that could be made? From our side, I mean?

PAULA: What!

LUC: Right, yes, and what if the fault lay with us? Hunh? In us? The entire fault ours alone? On our side it's all violins playing "If we only had love, we would melt all the guns. Then we'd give the new world. . ." Now is that what YOU WANT? (HE *imitates the sound of a romantic violin playing.*) Yadadadadah. But for them it's bulubulu. (*Imitating a medicine man doing a ritual.*) Just imagine, and if I take back my question and if they're right, even an itsy-bitsy bit right. . . Let's approach this scientifically. As if our situation was an amoeba or a mysterious chemical solution someone put under the microscope. . . Let's be self-analytical. . . If they're wrong, we can be all the more convinced of the injustice of it all, and if they're right, even if it's just by a micro-hair's breadth of one percent, that means we could improve by the micro-hair's breadth necessary! After all, who's perfect? And either way we win, don't we?

PAULA: I don't understand what you're saying at all.

LUC: I'm speaking scientifically.

PAULA: You believe what you're saying. Admit it! Yes you believe it!

LUC: There are worse things.

PAULA: Worse?

LUC: God's gift to humanity. Yes, they say you think you're god's gift to humanity. Who thinks they're better than anyone else. Not the wife in the kitchen doing the dishes. A phony, if you prefer. They see you as someone who sets herself two feet higher than all the rest. That's the image of you that's out there. Terrible, isn't it? Taking it all quite seriously, without trying to sweep it under the carpet, without the slightest bit of self-criticism. That's what they say. It's a painful accusation. Not very flattering for sure, but we can't just ignore it!

PAULA: That's how you see me!

LUC: No, no, and again no!

PAULA: You're lying.

LUC: Me lying? In point of fact you don't believe a word I say! I'm telling you that I'm suffering. Not that I don't love you, but that I'm suffering. Isn't that crystal clear? To me you're still my love, my one and only love. My love for now and always, and when a person's got such a love with violins going and so on, with you, I've got the whole world, it's for sure: You're Africa, authenticity, truth, my challenge. The challenge thanks to which I will become a man. She who will make me proud. But not only me, my son too. Yes, Nelson too—will be proud, not just a tiny bit proud, oh no, but all-the-way proud, fatally proud. . .

PAULA: Luc! What are you talking about? You're crazy! You're crazy!

LUC: . . . you're the whole world to me, I wouldn't call that into question, but, but, BUT, BUT. . . You see what I'm saying. . . BUT, BUT. . .

PAULA: But what?

LUC: But what? But what? That is the question.

*Silence.*

LUC: Intermission. Time out for commentary. It's healthy for couples to argue sometimes! It's important to get everything out in the open. Everything. It's like a hike in the mountains—hard but purifying.

PAULA: Stop! Talk! But what?

*Silence.*

LUC: But what? Intermission over. There's something else.

PAULA: . . .

LUC: Tacky.

PAULA: Tacky?

LUC: Your glad rags, your expensive hair-dos, your parades, your salsa, your make-up. . . it's seen as tacky. That's what they say.

PAULA: . . .

LUC: Tacky. . . It means bad taste. . . Tacky, tacky, tacky. You wear too much base, red on black, those doodads hanging from your ears, it's hideous. . . I know—you'll say you like them like that, but it doesn't go over and we've got to face it.

PAULA: How about you?

LUC: Besides, there was a shadow of a doubt. Let's not lie to ourselves, let's not beat around the bush, I used to like it all somehow. I did like it. . . but now I'm not so sure. Make up's for the benefit of the outside world, not for one's own benefit. . . True?

PAULA: And my clothes too?

LUC: Ah, your clothes! You really want to hear about "your clothes?"

PAULA: Yes.

LUC: Really?

PAULA: Yes.

LUC: No, I won't tell you.

PAULA: Tell me.

LUC: Well, they're awful.

PAULA: Awful?

LUC: Your tight-fitting pants, the neon colors. . . Your high heels. . . You mean those clothes?

PAULA: So?

LUC: You remind me of. . . no. . .

PAULA: Talk!

LUC: When I see them I think WHORE!

PAULA: . . .

LUC: Whore, prostitute, slut. . . That's what they say, that's what they say. . .

PAULA: They say that!

LUC: Well I don't! And then they go on to say: The worst of it's that she wore that stuff while she was pregnant. A pregnant whore!

PAULA: M. . .me?

LUC: "Me." And how about me? What am I supposed to tell them? Hunh? If you're the whore, what does that make me? Say it. I'm the PIMP. Pimp, that's the word for it.

PAULA *suddenly slaps* LUC.

LUC: Slap me, go ahead and slap me. Except you—you can afford not to care about it. You don't have their eyes glued on you. You're not from here. Do I tie myself in knots over what the people of your village might think of me when I look at a photo of them? Out of respect, maybe. . . but I wouldn't let myself go nuts over it, believe me! Here I'm the one who takes it all on the chin, Paula. They're my friends. It's my country. . .

PAULA: You think so too. You do.

LUC: People from here are discreet, the opposite of in Africa.

PAULA: You don't like my face. You don't like my skirt.

LUC: I always told you so! A little exoticism's fine, but not too much. If you don't make sure there's a balance. It tips over into being obscene. . .

PAULA: And when you first met me?

LUC: Scatology, pornography. . .

PAULA: At the disco, you saw me as one of those girls?

LUC: I'm talking about now.

PAULA: Here or back there, I'm the same person.

LUC: Now, then, no difference.

PAULA: You filthy-minded creep.

LUC: It's in their minds, not mine!

PAULA: You're an animal. . . A monster. I hate you. . .

LUC: I'm talking about what I'm going through. Me.

PAULA: *Yovo podi! Yovo podi!* [Dirty White!]

LUC: "Pygmalion," "My Fair Lady." You remember? You wanted to be somebody. Someone fine. A modern woman of the world! I believed you could. . .

PAULA *crosses away, hands on her belly.*

PAULA: (*Cry of pain.*) Ahaia, ahaia. . .

LUC: (*To himself.*) You wanted me to keep lying? Playing the part of the happy husband? What you really like is when I just shut up!

PAULA: (*Low.*) Nelson, Nelson!

LUC: Honesty has its price!

PAULA: *Ashao, ashao. . .* [Whore.]

LUC: Some truths hurt. But I can't lie. I had to tell you. You needed to know! How could you ever imagine that I saw you as a whore? How? Not for all the world! To me you're my wife, and my wife is sacred, not a whore! I'm only reporting what other people say! Other people! In their eyes you've become a whore. There's no getting away from it, and me your pimp, the most repulsive creature on earth! You think that makes me happy? We have to know, and we have to live with it. Was I wrong? The truth hurts?

PAULA: *Yakamé!* [Dirty louse!]

LUC: It hurts me too.

PAULA: *Yovo podi!*

LUC: It had to be discussed. . . Paula.

PAULA: *Yakamé.*

LUC: Paula?

PAULA *falls down prostrate.*

## SCENE ELEVEN
## "He's Yelling!"

*In the Parents' Studio Apartment.*

LUC *and* PAULA. *A giant mess.* PAULA *is in a weakened state, extremely nervous.* LUC *is seated in the center of the room.*

PAULA: (*Discomfited.*) He's crying. Can't you hear? He's crying!

*Silence.*

LUC: You want to go up and see?

*Silence.*

LUC: He's doing fine, believe me. Just fine. He likes taking his bath upstairs, and he gets along very well with my mother and with the maid too. It's to make things easier for you, Paula. Haven't you seen the condition you're in?

PAULA: I hear him, I'm telling you. I hear him.

*Silence.*

LUC: How about the doctor? (*Silence.*) The ethnopsychiatrist.

PAULA: . . .

LUC: You have such trouble understanding that all the problems you're having start in the head. The head! You're somatizing. Everyone's in agreement on that point. There's only one person who can give you the help you need.

*Silence.* LUC *starts to approach* PAULA, *who pulls back suddenly.*

LUC: God, how can she be so narrow-minded?

PAULA: . . .

LUC: And where's the partnership? I'm holding up my end!

PAULA: (*To herself.*) *Yovo podi, yovo podi. . .*

*Silence.*

LUC: (*More serious.*) This mess, all the dust, the odor. . . I made a mess of my bachelor pad in my time, but never to this extent. It's a scary situation for the child. We'll have problems with the N.O.C.

PAULA: . . . ?

LUC: The N-O-C. . . (*Quoting.*) In cases where recommendations fail to be followed and the child's household continues to reveal deficiencies regarding health and hygiene, The National Office of Children, on the basis of a recommendation from the inspector assigned to the case, has every right to take custody of the child either temporarily or permanently. In the event of parental resistance, he may have recourse, if necessary, to the police force. . .

PAULA: You're lying.

LUC: The N.O.C. handles all such inquiries.

PAULA: Liar!

LUC: Tell me what I'm supposed to do! I'm at the end of my rope. I've tried everything with you!

PAULA: I want to go away!!!

LUC: And if I asked you to stay?

PAULA: I want to go away with you.

LUC: What about the kid?

PAULA: Nigeria's the only way left.

LUC: We have to be realistic. A child in Africa is suicide! He'll take three steps and zap! He'll be chomped on by some mysterious mosquitoes or crunch, gobbled up and finished off from the inside by amoebas or some other vermin. Is that what you want?

PAULA: You tell me. Where you want to go.

LUC: Where I want to go?

PAULA: Where?

LUC: Where? (*The idea is: Nowhere.*) Money, money, money! It's over. End of the road! Don't you get it? We've run out of cards to play. Not now! Oh, later, maybe, later, sure. Just think if I become an international correspondent. You'll have a ring on every finger and a finger in every country. 2, 3, 10 kids, however many you want running around, all of them happy. Mommy dearest, daddy you're so handsome. . . Only, forget it. It ain't like that. It went haywire somewhere along the line. God only knows where. . .

## SCENE TWELVE
## "Paula's Dream"

*Mental Space.*

PAULA *alone with the baby.*

PAULA: All the others got killed by the hunters
He's been walking and walking through the furious wind and dried out brush
And a man came who was black and very tall
He came close and touched his eye
He stuck his finger deep down inside
But it didn't hurt
He touched his ears and the sound changed
Everything got quiet
The little lion didn't hear the furious wind anymore or the rifle shots, but the moss on the trees a flower in the desert buds a sprig of seaweed which spreads clear across the water
He was in the man's arms
But the man had changed
Now he had the wings of an eagle
He leaned over and now his mouth became a beak
He pulled out his tongue with the beak and in its place put a little snake
Then with his claws he opened up his belly and tore out his heart
And there he put a ball of fire
But when the ball of fire touched his belly it went out and turned cold and black
A piece of coal
The eagle flew off crying caw caw
The lion was now a beautiful big lion but he'd stopped moving

## SCENE THIRTEEN
## "Family Plot"

*Mental Space.*

SORCERER 1 *plays* THE GRANDMOTHER, SORCERER 2 THE MOTHER, *and* SORCERER 3 THE FATHER.

SORCERER 3 (FATHER): Wait my dear first we have to resolve the question of the child and then we'll think about the food allowance.
It's neither her character nor her origins
I repeat it's neither her character nor her origins which should be emphasized, but her behavior.
Show how unacceptable compared to what's considered a normal life in Belgium

SORCERER 2 (MOTHER): Pay attention to your father Luc we have to make an iron-clad case

SORCERER 3: We must gather together objective facts establishing that she doesn't take care of Albert or does it badly

SORCERER 1 (GRANDMOTHER): I'm sure she hits the child

SORCERER 3: Find witnesses, ask around to their friends

SORCERER 1: Albert doesn't always walk and I say it's because of her

SORCERER 3: Grandma please don't mix everything up

SORCERER 1: Not to mention she stinks

SORCERER 2: Yes she's not normal
Albert senses it and that's why he cries so much

SORCERER 3: De Wolf said that a psychiatric opinion would be best in this case

SORCERER 2: Oh, impossible
Poor baby she screams rape at the sight of anyone wearing a white lab coat

SORCERER 1: There must be black doctors

SORCERER 3: Careful shh not so loud shh

SORCERER 1: De Wolf's a good man

SORCERER 3: Son, we've got to put together an iron-clad case

SORCERER 2: And us such an open family
The problem's that you loved her too much
Your love blinded you
You couldn't see the evil she was harboring inside

SORCERER 1: With negro women it never works out

SORCERER 3: Grandma please

SORCERER 2: She's not going to get Albert
We'll have to fight
She has no rights over him
She who only wants to have fun dancing buying making herself up dressing sleeping feathering her nest

SORCERER 1: Feathering feathering feathering with a Belgian passport obviously

SORCERER 2: My poor Luc, do you think she might actually go out and get a job some day

SORCERER 3: If only she'd have helped you take photos

SORCERER 1: I've been saying all along—all she wants is a husband at her feet

SORCERER 2: Oh Luc, you've got to free yourself from her

SORCERER 3: Son, as sure as I'm your father, we'll get you through this mess
An iron-clad case to establish the fact that she fails in her maternal duties
Say at the day-care center they can testify to that can't they

SORCERER 2: Who takes Albert to the day-care center every morning who goes to pick him up gives him food
Who dresses him who takes care of him when he's sick who who who on the other hand I know exactly
Who lets him cry and who pretends she's the only one trying to protect him
That insane liar and manipulator

SORCERER 3: Ah the psychiatrist
How do we go about getting her to see a psychiatrist
Force her
Trick her into it

SORCERER 2: And what secrets might be lurking in that hairdressing salon she spends so much time in

SORCERER 1: She whose hair is falling out

SORCERER 2: Yvonne hah the great Yvonne that's alright with me
But if she had a lover besides

SORCERER 3: Ah a lover
Interesting
That would make quite an impact in the trial like a burglary or any other crime
You think that she might be drugging Luc

SORCERER 2: Let her get out of Belgium if it's not good enough for her

SORCERER 1: Yes let her get out of Belgium is too good for her

SORCERER 3: Let her get out but without Albert

## SCENE FOURTEEN
## "The Scissors"

*In the Parents' Studio Apartment.*

LUC *and* PAULA.

LUC: It's true what mama says
If she hadn't walked into the bathroom at that moment
Tell me yes or no if it's important yes or no
How could I love you after such an abominable act
You are the most despicable of women
To drown what was in your own belly
You take him in your arms to give him a bath
And you lower him into the water until he's immersed in water all the way

Gently under water
Not a sound no crying
In just a few seconds it's all over
He's so little
May your belly cause you pain
Yes suffer and suffer some more
Oh why didn't you try it on me
Confess you didn't have the courage
I'm going to show you what it's like to have courage
Show you what you deserve
You wanted to kill yourself with shiny scissors
Well you see those two blades spotless for now
You're going to make a place for them
Yes a little gap between your bones
Offer the scissor blades a bloody sheath to enter
In order to make you remember deep down in your very own guts what such an act really means
Unless you slice yourself even deeper, right down to the bloodiest, blackest part of yourself
So that you never pull that again or even think of killing striking and don't even think of touching petting caressing my son yes my son or even listen to me even trying to be in his presence getting close to him to my son only to me no never again I swear you'll never see him again

PAULA: Luc

LUC: (*Stopped in the middle of a lethal blow.*) What

PAULA: Let me see Nelson

LUC: You're lucky I'm too good
I could never be your murderer
Even if you'd done the worst possible I could never murder you

PAULA: I'm leaving I'll never see him again

LUC: Yes yes leave tomorrow I'll buy the ticket they're going to file a complaint you know and the police will come
The shame of it all
What am I going to tell them
I'll hold them back for now you've got to leave yes now

PAULA: Nelson is your son Luc don't let them touch him I'm sure he'll die
*Miabé lonlon lé soyi mavo* [Our love will last till the end of time.]
Aaaaaaie the eyes they keep coming back I see the eyes
Who are all of them there
*Soyi mavo* [The end of time.]
Get away get away don't look at me
Those eyes all around me turning to white
*Yama yama*

LUC: You're hallucinating.

PAULA: Go away with Nelson you've got to go away from here
*N'tsanwo lé N'suwo dome* [You are the best of all men.]

LUC: Paula, stop it, stop it.

PAULA *loses consciousness.* LUC *touches her midriff and withdraws his hands soaked with blood.*

## SCENE FIFTEEN
## "In the Cemetery"

*Several months have passed.* LUC *runs onstage, pushing a stroller.* THE SORCERERS *all participate in creating the imaginary voice(s) of* NELSON *in the stroller.*

SORCERERS: Vroom vroom faster daddy weeeeh more more slow down
Watch out dodge hop
Yeah, upsy and we're off
You're in good shape that'll make her happy
Vroooom faster daddy that was good on the curve.
On just two wheels yay
You can be sure she can see us
Behind the row right at the end of the path tomb number 14 is there
Floor it.
The first time this year
To the bottom, bottom bottom I hope nothing's changed
To the bottom daddy I said
Why are you stopping
Cheer up daddy you promised me
Don't talk nonsense you know we've got to do it
Daddy daddy

LUC: Because you do as I say
I listen to you
Do you do what I tell you
Come on talk to me
Smile hold onto me kick your feet

SORCERERS (*Yelling*)
Mommy I want to see mommy let me see mommy
You promised me Daddy
I want to see mommy

LUC: Shh quiet now Nelson
Nelson don't cry
That's my good Nelson
If you want to see mommy you'll see her
But only on condition that you listen to me
That you eat tonight

SORCERERS: (*Yelling.*) Mom-my, mom-my

LUC: You're doing that on purpose Nelson stop crying
You should never cry
Either you walk or you don't walk
If you take that tone with me I won't walk
Shh people are staring at us because of you
They're going to think there's something wrong with me
(*Justifying himself to invisible passers-by.*)
Everything's fine
That's life
I'm talking to myself in a cemetery
What can you do
Life isn't always easy
Yes hello
To you too
(*Same business as before.*)
You want to go back to
You like it so much there I guess
I'm the one who decides where you go and don't forget it
No no Nelson don't do that
I know you understand what I'm saying
Yes yes what do you expect
I know you
I know you very well
So don't pull that with me

SORCERERS: (*Yelling louder.*) Mom-my, mom-my
Mom-my, mom-my
Mom-my, mom-my

LUC: Okay, okay

SORCERERS: (*Yelling loud.*) Mom-my mom-my

LUC: Okay, I said okay I give up
Shhh shhhh shhh

SORCERERS: (*Softer.*) Mom-my mom-my

LUC: I understood Nelson
Nelson don't yell

SORCERERS: (*Softly.*) Mom-my mom-my

LUC: You want to see her you'll see her

SORCERERS: (*Enthusiastically.*) I'm here mommy with Daddy

LUC: You can say whatever you like
To your mommy little one
Of course she can hear you even under that rock
What can you do with big people that's the way it is sometimes
No she's not taking a nap but she can't get out
That's just the way it is
But we have to listen to her too
Listen to her
You hear her
Listening to her's important

**CURTAIN**

# PATRIOT'S CAFÉ

by

JEAN-MARIE PIEMME

## CAST

(*In order of appearance*)

Loulou, *young guy, out of work*

Yvonne, *waitress at the Patriot's Café*

Julian, *young guy, out of work, friend of Carmen's*

Carmen, *waitress, friend of Julian's*

Willy DeWolf, *proprietor of the Patriot's Café, member of the National Front*

Gianni Gorda, *journalist, friend of Claudia's*

Freddy, *Willy's man of all work*

Leopold Lesca, *businessman, with connections to the Extreme Right*

Claudia, *Yvonne's daughter*

Man in Exile

Minister of the Interior

Guest 1

Guest 2

Simon Florkin, *former member of the Resistance*

## PART ONE

### SCENE ONE

*Patriot's Café.* YVONNE, *one of the waitresses, and* LOULOU, *a young kid who occasionally pitches in at the café. It is getting close to closing time.*

LOULOU: What you tell the police?

YVONNE: Nothing. They were wearing hoods.

LOULOU: Then it's a miracle you're still alive.

YVONNE: I'm a Pisces. Horoscope says it's a lucky day for Pisces. And I believe in that stuff. I believe in it with all my heart and soul.

LOULOU: And I bet your whole life passed before your eyes.

YVONNE: Nope. Didn't.

LOULOU: But they say that at the moment of your death, your whole life passes before your eyes.

YVONNE: Blondie's the one who'd know if that were true or not. He's the one they went for. Bam, in his face. Went off right between his eyes. And then I saw all that blood. And in my head, the same stuff kept playing over and over: Is there as much blood in a little body as a big one? Is there as much blood in a little body as a big one? Is there as. . .

LOULOU: That's whack.

YVONNE: They'll live to regret it. He who sows the wind will reap the whirlwind.

LOULOU: And you didn't see *any*thing?

YVONNE: Their teeth obviously! They didn't give a shit about the money. But blood and guts, oh yeah! Animals! Wolves!

LOULOU: Doesn't make sense, any of it. A cartload of people dead on the floor, and all that money just lying there.

YVONNE: Same as the last time. You feel like you'd committed some terrible sin.

LOULOU: Yvonne, you got courage. Just like Willy says all the time: That Yvonne's one fearless broad.

YVONNE: Willy says that? Everybody knows him around here. The hoodlums outside the café keep their heads down as they walk past. But people who need to get hold of him know where to find him. That's for sure. Okay. Let's close up. Tomorrow, right on time! Punctuality is next to godliness.

LOULOU: Yeah. Everybody does the best they can.

LOULOU *exits. Enter* JULIAN.

JULIAN: Carmen around?

YVONNE: You again?

YVONNE *goes into the back room.* CARMEN *comes out.* SHE *notices* JULIAN.

CARMEN: What do you want? I told you never to set foot in here.

JULIAN: Come over here. (HE *tries to kiss* HER. SHE *pulls away, feebly, but still.*) Carmen, you don't love me anymore, is that what you're trying to tell me?

CARMEN: It's not true!

JULIAN: You don't love me!

CARMEN: I do too.

JULIAN: When love is over, it's better for all concerned to come out and admit that it's over.

CARMEN: I don't got nothing. You can't love somebody when you don't got nothing. I'm one step above a bag-lady. You know what a bag-lady is? She ain't a queen, that's for sure. People just barely graze their hands over her pussy real careful. And they forget she exists very, very, very, fast.

JULIAN: I want you.

CARMEN: And how am I supposed to pay the rent?

JULIAN: The rent! Why do you talk to me about rent? Let's drink to a second-rate life, that's what you really mean. Are you supposed to go through your whole life just so you can pay the rent? What about the gates of heaven? And awesome ideas? And lifting yourself up by your bootstraps out of the slime you were born in? And standing out? A person who you see always looking down, he's already dead. You need to remember that!

CARMEN: In the meantime, a fistful of bills in between your thighs is a hell of a lot more satisfying than getting your neck sliced off by the grim reaper's scythe, if you see what I mean.

JULIAN: I come from good stock. I don't want it to be just about the shopping cart piled with food for the weekend. Or a shiny Mercedes. Or the hand you can never get clean. I don't want to live my life as a mouth scarfing stuff down. There are so many things to accomplish in life, Carmen! Doing something big. Becoming somebody. Shining down through the memory of time. Doesn't that count for anything? I have all that in me and more, I can feel it. Otherwise I might as well throw myself into the ocean. I'm twenty years old. I despise mediocrity. Mediocrity gives me the creeps.

CARMEN: Those words come shooting out of your mouth, and they go off around my head like fireworks. And then after, everything's the same as before.

JULIAN: Would you like me to be a nothing?

CARMEN: I've had it up to here with your bullshit. I've got holes in my sweater. My bra's all pulled out of shape and every day I bathe in the same damn ooze. Have you ever seen my mother? You get old real quick when all you've got is nothing. And you turn bad, real bad. She was beautiful, my mother, in the old days. Alive, happy!

JULIAN: Carmen, stay with me.

CARMEN: Desire's just an animal.

JULIAN: Carmen. . .

CARMEN: I love you Julian. It's going to hurt a lot, but there's nothing we can do about it. We've been forced into this position. Just once in my life, I'd like to prance around on a white horse. Why shouldn't I have the right?

JULIAN: Without you there, what'll become of me? I'd go kaboom into a thousand pieces. I'd shrivel up.

HE *rushes at her,* HE *kisses* HER, SHE *kisses* HIM, *pushes* HIM *away.*

CARMEN: Get the hell out of here, cretin! You think it's so easy? Get the hell out of here! Move it!

JULIAN *exits.* YVONNE *reenters, dressed for going out.*

YVONNE: I'm leaving. Double lock the door. And the alarm. Don't forget the alarm.

WILLY *enters, having come from the apartment over the café.*

WILLY: What's happening?

CARMEN: Nothing.

YVONNE: See you tomorrow, boss.

YVONNE *exits.*

WILLY: If anyone gives you any trouble, just call me.

CARMEN: Okay Willy. (HE *gets ready to go back upstairs.*) Willy?

WILLY: What?

CARMEN: Do you still want to?

WILLY: Want to what?

CARMEN: It was stupid of me. I didn't mean to slap you.

WILLY: Yeah, I still want to.

CARMEN: It'll cost you big-time.

WILLY: It'll cost whatever it costs, but when I want something, I want it. Tell me what'd make you happy.

CARMEN: To go away. Travel. See other sights.

WILLY: Sure. Yvonne'll take care of things while we're away.

CARMEN: I don't want people looking at me in the street anymore and thinking, that one there, all she's got going for her is her skin. She's gonna get old and withered real quick.

WILLY: I'll give you mouth to mouth. I don't like just sitting, watching gorgeous flowers going to shit.

WILLY *kisses* CARMEN, *puts his hand on her buttocks.*

CARMEN: Willy, I'll try. Really and truly, I'm gonna try. But it's gotta happen in its own good time—over time. When I want. When it feels right to me.

## SCENE TWO

*The street at night in front of the café.* GIANNI GORDA *strolls by.* JULIAN *is waiting, fast frozen, chilled to the bone.* HE *seems not to have gotten any sleep for several days.*

GORDA: Got a light? What the fuck you doing out here? Trying to commit suicide by freezing to death?

JULIAN: I'm waiting for a girl.

GORDA: Haven't seen any. Not a soul out on the avenue this time of night. Ghosts, sure, they're plenty of them around. But a real soul, don't hold your breath.

JULIAN: Her name's Carmen, mister.

GORDA: What do you want me to do about it? They're all called Carmen!

JULIAN: She's been gone for three days now.

GORDA: Three days, don't get bent out of shape. She'll be back. Three days, think of it as a longish time-out. They go off for three days and then they come back, and they go down on their knees and they say, "Forgive me, I just had to." And they cry. God knows why, but they gotta cry. They go away, they come back, they cry. That's just the way it goes. And all that time, you're back there spending your evening snug as a bug in a rug with Johnny Walker.

JULIAN: Your woman ever leave you?

GORDA: No way, sonny!

JULIAN: Then how come you look so out of it?

GORDA: My woman's made of concrete, a regular queen if you get my point. If I go out at night, it's because she's back there in that bed, lying warm and cozy with her eyes lulled to sleep and beauty stamped deep into her face. And meanwhile, I can't close my eyes. So's not to wake her up, I walk the streets in silence, trying not to talk to myself because Claudia's hyper-sensitive, and I know she'd hear me out here, even though she's asleep. You believe what I'm telling you or you just pretending? Motherfucking world! There's always some little cretin out there who'll stare at you with his eyes popping out of his kisser. Well, you don't know who you're looking at, 'cause if you knew your eyes'd pop out twice as far, and you'd say, fuck, that's *him*! It was *him* I bumped into tonight! Too bad on you, 'cause you got the eyes of a dog who don't know his own master. Go ahead, beat it. Then it'll be just the same as it always is—me walking along, incognito in silence. Sorry, I haven't seen your little chickadee pecking at the pavement, but don't let it get you down kid, 'cause the Almighty always says: Seek and ye shall find! Take it light!

## SCENE THREE

*Patriot's Café. Room off the bar.* CARMEN *enters.* SHE *has made a large number of purchases.*

CARMEN: Willy?

YVONNE: Not here.

CARMEN: He hasn't gotten back yet?

YVONNE: Better believe it.

CARMEN: The sky is smiling down, the streets are swarming with people. I could have bought up the entire store. Want to see?

YVONNE: I've got work to do.

CARMEN: Yvonne, what did I do?

YVONNE: Nothing.

CARMEN: Since we got back from Egypt, you don't talk to me anymore.

YVONNE: Should I carry the packages up to the apartment?

CARMEN: I can do it myself.

YVONNE: Here's Willy.

WILLY *enters.*

CARMEN: How do I look? Like it? Don't I look good? Will ya look at that face on you. You look like you just saw a corpse.

WILLY: Don't say that, goddammit! Don't laugh at me, Carmen. There I am with the arraigning judge, and I want to say to him: You have any idea how much time I've spent cooling my heels here already? Ain't justice grand!!! Ain't it efficient!!! And at that very moment, I realize I'd just lost a tooth. It fell out. Crap, right down my throat! So there I am sticking my fingers all the way in, but I'd already swallowed it. The arraigning judge is there staring at me. You can imagine what I must have looked like, and I start talking again. But it was rough. I only had one thing in my head—why'd that rotten tooth have to fall out right then. *Why*? A thing like that could only happen to me! Can you see anything?

CARMEN: No, nothing.

WILLY: What do you mean, nothing? I just lost a tooth.

YVONNE: That's right, there's a space there.

CARMEN: Not serious.

WILLY: Don't you understand what it means to have a tooth drop out of your mouth?

CARMEN: We've all got thirty-two.

WILLY: Is she blind or something? It smells to high heaven of a jinx. Rotten luck guaranteed. I guess I gotta paint you the whole picture: First a tooth loosens, next thing, bang, your heart gives out. Then the coffin. There's a widow! Jig's up! Some joke! And this has to hit me *now*, of all times!

YVONNE: Give me your jacket. I'm going to go get you something.

WILLY: Fucking arraigning judge!

CARMEN: What did he want with you?

WILLY: My chick. My very own little chick, I didn't even give you your kiss yet.

*Kiss, which irritates* YVONNE.

YVONNE: That won't bring us back the Congo!

SHE *exits.*

WILLY: A beagle with a kisser like a Jew. A government bureaucrat, that's him to a tee! Mister DeWolf, what exactly do you know about these assassination attempts? Nothing, Your Honor, I don't know anything about any assassination attempts. I do got very definite opinions about the society we live in. That don't mean I'm a gunman. I've got nothing to do with the kind of guys who go around shooting people, Your Honor. I own a bar, and everybody knows it: Willy's place, the Patriot's Café. Why don't you go straight to my bar and ask anyone there exactly where to find the guilty parties. And the victims too, while you're at it. Go right ahead!

YVONNE: (SHE *comes back with two glasses of beer.*) Here we are!

WILLY *downs them both.*

WILLY: Beer's like women. You gotta down 'em just like that, while they're still nice and fresh! (HE *laughs.*) You see the face she's making? Look at it. Just look at that face she's making! You ok, Yvonne? Ah, you just don't like my jokes. You think I'm a low-life.

YVONNE: There's someone waiting to see you.

WILLY: Who?

YVONNE: He came several times while you were away on vacation. At the counter. A big guy with a face like a pork butcher. (WILLY *exits.*) Willy's like water in the desert. People can't get enough of it. I do the best I can, but I'm the kind of person can't be more than one place at a time. Of course I'm not blaming you Carmen, but this morning some flowers came for you.

CARMEN: Who?

YVONNE: Roses.

CARMEN: What of it?

YVONNE: Whatever you do with Willy is none of my business. And whatever you do with any of them others—that's none of my business either. I'll go get them.

SHE *goes out and comes back with an enormous bouquet.*

CARMEN: They're beautiful.

YVONNE: Considering what they go for these days, the guy who sent them must dig you a lot, that's for sure!

CARMEN *detaches a card, reads it, hides it discreetly inside her blouse when* WILLY *returns followed by* A BIG GUY, *a primitive mass, brutal and obscene, just raring to jump on the horns of any woman who comes along.*

WILLY: It's Freddy. He was trying to find me. The sheet metal plant: Sorry, not hiring. The research institute: No, not qualified. Civil service: Oh no, no connections. The store for fine threads: Er, uh, not the type they're looking for. So I pop over to your place. And what do I say? Sure thing, buddy! Here's my hand, let's shake on it. Come over here, Freddy.

CARMEN: How about me? Aren't you going to introduce me?

WILLY: My little chick, my Carmen.

FREDDY: (*Singsong, trying to get on* CARMEN*'s good side.*) There once was a Spaniard from Brussels, her snatch, it was loaded with mussels. . .

CARMEN *bursts out laughing.*

YVONNE: Mind your manners, young man!

FREDDY: The boss likes horsing around too, right, boss?

WILLY: You know it. Yvonne, get that little room on the third floor ready for him.

FREDDY: Thanks boss.

WILLY: Hey! (*Holds a fistful of bills out to* HIM.) Tomorrow, eight o'clock, be ready for the job.

FREDDY: Eight o'clock with bells on, boss.

YVONNE *and* FREDDY *exit.*

WILLY: That's the way I am. (HE *points at the flowers.*) What's that?

CARMEN: I was about to tell you. They're from the guy who got there before you. But you've got no reason to go ballistic. His sending them's totally clean and aboveboard.

WILLY: Oh yeah?

CARMEN: He's some kind of philosopher, if you see what I mean. Now what would *I* ever do with a philosopher, I ask you? In the first place, all his babbling doesn't thrill me. He's always been that way—s'got his head in the clouds. And then out of the blue, he sends you flowers. Besides, all he ever talks is that philosophy crap. You say to him, I dig you, and he comes back with the Nature of Heaven, the Absolute, Human Responsibility, and a long rigamarole about some kind of caverns, from morning to night. So then, I suppose he must have wanted to stop by here, but I unfortunately wasn't around. I say unfortunately because I wouldn't have minded getting one more look at him. You know, like that, for one hot minute. I'm sure you like seeing your exes from time to time. I would have been able to show him the kind of person I've become, and all because of what you pay me. Cinderella right before the clock strikes twelve. If you want me to, I'll just throw 'em out. Why not? Just say the word and into the wastebasket they go. Don't even have to say anything. The slightest little twitch, and boop! And anyway, look here on the little cardboard card. All it says is Julian. My name isn't even there. That means he must have already forgotten it. I can just see him thinking to himself: today's just the right day for that girl whose name I don't remember. He's like that. He twists everything around. He mixes everything up. So what I'm trying to say is, there's no real reason why we should throw out the flowers. After all, they dress the place up, they smell good. . . And anyway, I wouldn't like you to bring those big elephant paws of yours down on me like I was some can of beer or something. You are what you are, but there are certain lines you just can't cross. So if a guy like you started making a big scene over a lousy flower just because some little pipsqueak with his head in the clouds stopped by when I wasn't even here, well, I might just take it the wrong way, see? I was getting all upset over nothing because, between him and me, there's not even any electric current running. You follow?

WILLY: Carmen, let's get married. If you want, we can get married.

CARMEN: That's not exactly the point I was trying to make, Willy.

WILLY: I want the whole shmear: The church, the white dress, the ring, the red carpet, the maids of honor.

CARMEN: That's nice Willy.

WILLY: We'll be respectable. Mister and Missis. You'll be my wife. I'm not just some kind of creep who lets himself get sucked off by any old piece of ass.

CARMEN: Very refined, I'm sure.

WILLY: So what are you waiting for? Put the flowers in a vase.

CARMEN: The vase is a good solution as far as the flowers are concerned. But as for you and me walking down the aisle, there I'm not so sure. You must be feeling a little light-headed or something, 'cause I can't exactly see myself in that picture. You're weird so *much* lately, like some old airplane that's starting to get cracks all over. My ass isn't enough for you? Look at it. Isn't having it there in your hands enough for you? Isn't it hot enough for you? You've got to start fantasizing about grand organs and wedding marches?

WILLY: You don't like the idea?

CARMEN: I think I'll think it over very carefully, if you don't have any problem with that.

WILLY: How about giving me an advance?

CARMEN: Yeah, I think I like you better that way!

HE *grabs* HER *just at the moment when* FREDDY *comes back in.* FREDDY *looks at* THE COUPLE *making out, then after a moment.*

FREDDY: Boss, you said eight o'clock with bells on.

## SCENE FOUR

LEOPOLD LESCA *is coming back home late at night.*

LESCA: Julian? Where are you? This house is more barren than a desert.

JULIAN *enters.* HE *has changed. Cleaner. Neater.*

JULIAN: Is that you sir?

LESCA: Like in the Gospels, I'm the wicked disciple who fell asleep.

JULIAN: What's going on?

LESCA: They're falling all over themselves trying to figure out how to get me. They're hounding me.

JULIAN: Around midnight the telephone rang several times, but I didn't answer, just like you told me.

LESCA: The slander is starting up all over again.

JULIAN: Who?

LESCA: The mental midgets. The mental midgets who harbor rancor in their hearts. And haven't got an idealistic bone in their bodies. Listen, Julian. I'm a straight arrow. If you ever hear any malicious talk about me, swear to me that you won't believe it. Swear.

JULIAN: I swear.

LESCA: Yesterday they all got in a long line to shake my hand. In their electoral campaigns or in their business dealings my services came in very handy. They called me "Leopold—friend!" "My best friend Leopold." Today they drag my name through the mud, with a miserable trial. You'll never be ungrateful, will you?

JULIAN: No, sir.

LESCA: Ingratitude is the gall of the opportunist, a vice proper to the low wage-earner. A man with a big heart ought never bow before it.

JULIAN: Mister Lesca, I know how much I'm in your debt. I was being pulled in by the undertow. It was so bad, I had fish swimming in my hair. When all of a sudden an arm appears to pull me out of the water. Your arm.

LESCA: Without me, you'd still be down there today. That's quite correct!

JULIAN: You welcome me into your house. Here I eat, sleep. You take me in hand, you give me books to read. . .

LESCA: Have you read "The Essay on the Inequality of the Human Races" as I'd suggested?

JULIAN: Not yet, sir.

LESCA: Why not? You must obey me in all things. Since the dawn of time there's been a mission which is now ours to fulfill. To arrest the free-fall. The blood used to be pure. Inequality of the races corrupted that purity. We've got to be ready. To put a stop to the decadent downward slide into slime. Standing tall. In place. Bolt upright. Perhaps even to stride joyously to our deaths, for proximity to death is the one thing in the world that can lend things any meaning.

JULIAN: Excuse me, but I don't want to read that book.

LESCA: It's your duty. Your race, your exalted race imposes that duty on you. Where are your claws? Where are your teeth?

JULIAN: I don't have any.

LESCA: And a man, tell me—what is he?

JULIAN: A man. . . a man. . .

LESCA: Is not a man simply a constant tension toward the infinite? Does it thrill you to hear me talk like that? You're asking yourself, what does that lousy phraseologist want with me? Does he think he's going to teach me how to live? Yes indeed, my friend! Oh yes! Life is a hatchet, and I'm going to bury it deep in your head! And the more mastery he gains, the more pleasure the student will take in giving pleasure.

JULIAN: Exactly. I've got a news flash for you—I've started to write a book.

LESCA: A book?!

JULIAN: A big book, a beautiful book. Chapter 1: Analysis of the mediocrity of this nation we're living in. A real slap in the face. I know you're going to love it. I want to pillory the junk that's cluttering up all the little minds. Where'd I put my note pad? In my pants pocket. Would you hand it to me?

LESCA: Young man, you have the effrontery of a young dog.

JULIAN: I'm telling you, it's dynamite.

LESCA: Fine! Fine! It's a scoop! We'll go all out for the scoop. Here's to the scoop! Long live scoops!

JULIAN *reads a few lines in his note pad.*

JULIAN: Down with the reign of all that's second-rate! Say no to compromise! What does the world of today amount to? A slap in the face? It's the empowered element that drives a nation. The lizard's tail of weakness must be cut off! (*Stops.*) Now that, that's not so bad, is it? (LESCA *remains impassive.* JULIAN *resumes.*) All it takes is for us to retrieve our spiritual energy from deep down in the mud and we'll shoot up to the sky if. . . if. (HE *stops, hesitates.*) You know, Carmen. . .

LESCA: What about Carmen?

JULIAN: I like the hair she's got under her arms.

LESCA: Carmen's underarm hair? I wonder if I myself would be absolutely immune to Carmen's underarm hair? What is "The Essay on the Inequality of the Races" to this Carmen's underarm hair?

JULIAN: Her belly is warm. It smells, it's good.

LESCA: She's not there for you anymore.

JULIAN: She's the most precious thing in the world to me.

LESCA: She threw you out. How long are going to live with a ghost?

JULIAN: You never saw her. How could you understand?

LESCA: It's so true, deep down inside of each being lurks an imbecility that we'll never quite dispense with. In vain do I extract these cells of stupidity from you one by one, for they simply grow back like a cancer.

JULIAN: Just look. (*Photo of* CARMEN.) Now do you understand?

LEOPOLD LESCA *barely looks at the photo.*

LESCA: Goret, I should have left you in the mud where I found you.

JULIAN: You don't have the right to speak to me like that.

LESCA: I ask pardon. I keep directing all my spitefulness at you. I'm clumsy. Life ages us dreadfully quickly. We become unjust, turn rancid like bad wine. And just look at how stupid one can get: I have all the vitality of youth before my very eyes, and what do I do? Turn up my nose at it. Your hands are innocent. It's not the miserable pittance you manage to save up day by day which really matters, but the gift you are to yourself. This I know. You're not stingy with your own person. Your eyes are starved for grandeur. The desire to stand out, a desire I know so well. I can drive you. I can make you into a soldier for the truth. Do you want me to? Do you want to be a useful man? Useful to himself, useful to the spirit of humanity? Do you want to?

JULIAN: I want to, I do.

LESCA: Then help me.

JULIAN: How?

LESCA: And if I demand your strength? All your strength? The stables must be cleaned out yet again. I'm talking about this country. Hunh, if you can call these scraps of people floating about in their own dereliction a country. Country!!! Are you never sickened when you walk down the street? Can't you just feel the defeat? And the drabness, oh, the drabness! The white man is a corpse. Where is the energy? Where? Abdication of man before his race. Me, I'm run to the ground. Just suppose you're high up on a cloud. You look down, what do you see?

JULIAN: I don't know.

LESCA: A nation without fire? A state emasculated? Yes! I say that we are a people dragging ourselves along on our knees, because between the ambient mess and the rampant collectivism, there's no sky left, no vital thought possible. But I'm standing vigil! I am standing vigil! How could we think of sleep if the glance of one being caressed our forehead, one soul being placed higher than we? What would we be without the discernment of God who has cast some into poverty and others into affluence? And you, whose hand I feel trembling, what would you be without me, little boy, when deep in your eyes I see all the indecision of the entire world? (JULIAN *is distraught.* HE *picks up the photo of* CARMEN *once more.*) Romeo sitting by the pond—whiles away his time dreaming of Juliet's charms even as my arm throws open the stable door, liberating a stench so bad it could bring tears to our eyes?

JULIAN: You're the devil, aren't you?

LESCA: Fling that down over there! I've had it up to here with your schoolboy fantasies! Strangle them! I don't want to see that photo ever again. Get rid of it!

JULIAN *tears up the photo.*

JULIAN: Sir, I have obeyed you.

LESCA: She is dead. It was the picture of a dead woman.

## SCENE FIVE

YVONNE*'s home.* CLAUDIA *has just arrived.* LOULOU *is putting on his jacket to go out.*

YVONNE: Loulou, pick out some really good stuff.

LOULOU: (*Ironic.*) Yeah, yeah. Good champagne's better than a kick in the ass.

YVONNE: Here, take thirty bucks.

CLAUDIA: Mama! That wasn't necessary!

YVONNE: What do you mean, not necessary!

CLAUDIA: We just dropped by to say hello. We're not staying.

YVONNE: I'm glad. A daughter is a part of her mother, and you should never forget that. No more arguments between us. Once and for all.

CLAUDIA: They're forgotten. Banished, done away with!

YVONNE: Dropping by without calling first. Do people drop by without any warning? I could have made something. And where is he? On the throne already? He's all the time on the throne.

CLAUDIA: Gianni has a stomach ache.

YVONNE: Stomach ache? He's already drunk, that's what's happening!

CLAUDIA: No, mom!

YVONNE: Excuse me for saying this, dear, but he's not the man for you. There, I said it, and now I'll shut up. Out in the world there's nothing but fighting and quarreling, but in this home we have a peaceful refuge.

LOULOU *returns with the champagne.*

LOULOU: Yvonne? Yvonne? I found some!

YVONNE: Yay, Loulou. Open it while I go get some glasses.

CLAUDIA *remains there alone with* LOULOU. *She takes a c.d. out of her bag and puts it in the player.*

CLAUDIA: It's Miles Davis. You like?

LOULOU: How about you, you like accordion music?

CLAUDIA: You been here a long time?

LOULOU: A few days. I'm sleeping in your bed. I mean, in your bedroom. (*Laughter.*)

CLAUDIA: Steer clear of her lectures!

LOULOU: She's already started! I wouldn't be surprised if she comes in and tucks me into bed.

YVONNE *comes back in.* SHE *immediately turns down the sound.*

YVONNE: Black music.

CLAUDIA: They've got more talent than any white man you mean.

YVONNE: Loulou didn't have anyplace to live. So I told him, my boy, you can have my daughter's room. He comes from Charleroi. "Oh dear old Charleroi, that's where I want to be. . ." Hey Loulou? True, it's not the Riviera. Fortunately he's still got his grandmother, but he doesn't want to live there. And here, he's looking for work. Willy helps him out from time to time.

LOULOU: Yvonne tells me I got to show what a responsible guy I am in order to impress Willy, and then maybe some day he'll make me a partner. (*Laughter.*)

YVONNE: The shirt humanity wears is very dirty. But a smile and a friendly hand can go a long way to making it a little cleaner.

GIANNI GORDA *enters.*

GORDA: What kind of bullshit is that? Are there any ashtrays in this house?

YVONNE: I'll go get you one! I'm going! Just wait and see, any minute now he's going to pee in my geraniums!

CLAUDIA: Leave him the hell alone, mom!

GORDA *exits.*

LOULOU: You're pretty different from each other, aren't you?

YVONNE: Deep down we're the same.

LOULOU: So long as you think so.

YVONNE: You usually imagine you see the most basic things, but in reality you can't see them at all. There are thousands of things all around us that go to prove it. Obviously, you've got to live according to rules. One: Never talk politics. Two: Don't talk about what I do or what you do. Three: Avoid all subjects that are too private. Oh, that reminds me, I've got a message for you. Pierrot stopped by. He said he wants to get back together with you.

CLAUDIA: No.

YVONNE: He's your husband

CLAUDIA: He's an asshole!

LOULOU: Hatchet bam in the forehead, and Pierrot's scalped.

YVONNE: You've put horns on your husband. You erase your father from memory. And your mother, her you shove right out of your life.

CLAUDIA: I do my best.

YVONNE: What a mouth on her!

LOULOU: See what's coming next!

YVONNE: And that mouth smeared with all that lipstick! With that damp body of yours you spark desire in men's bellies—all men. I've got to put up with you posting "Free Tibet" stickers everywhere and with the fact that the ozone layer's more important to you than your own mother; or that you throw your life away going to meetings to explain why the world has to be chopped in two! But when you start opening your mouth to tell me about *my friends*, there I draw the line! Willy isn't who you say he is. Among the Flemish, yes, I'm sure there are people like that. Racists. But not here in this part of the country. Willy is always good to whoever deserves it. And even those who deserve it he yells at. When Willy talks, I listen. He says, there are too many foreigners here, and I can understand what he's talking about. That's not racism. It's all about labor.

LOULOU: Yvonne, a finger of champagne please? Let the sparks fly!

YVONNE: (*Pointing at* HER DAUGHTER.) Why should I let you determine how I should live?

LOULOU: The atmosphere is charged!

CLAUDIA: All you see is Willy DeWolf's charming smile. We look over our shoulder, and the landscape we see isn't pretty. All the National Front and all those other extreme right organizations stand for is blood and destruction. Just between us, where would Hitler have been if he didn't have fine, upstanding people like you on his side?

LOULOU: Go ahead, give her what-for. That merits a response.

YVONNE: All I can say is that she's scum and that she goes around with scum, and anyone can see that!

CLAUDIA: A dying dog she'd give mouth-to-mouth resuscitation to, but when it comes to vast masses of people, she washes her hands of the whole situation!

GORDA, *who has overheard* CLAUDIA*'s remark, reenters.*

GORDA: It's not right, Mama Yvonne!

YVONNE: The dog can bark all it wants, but the convoy keeps right on going.

GORDA: Yvonne, I've got a good recipe for a cocktail. You want it?

YVONNE: I don't want anything from you!

GORDA: Three parts alcohol and one finger cirrhosis of the liver. And on the bottom of the glass, one lone drop of bitterness. (*Sings.*)
This old world has never changed,
And we are nothing, let's just be nothing.

LOULOU: There's something funny about the way you look. You might say that your whole body is structured around your nose.

GORDA: I like sniffing around. In a past life I must have been a dog.

LOULOU: You believe in that stuff?

GORDA: And do you believe in a guy like me whose favorite thing in the world is the smell of toilets? And now I've managed to pick up the scent of all these assassination attempts.

LOULOU: (*Singing low.*) "When a policeman in the police station laughs, all the police in the police station laugh along."

YVONNE: That's a lie! Aren't I the widow of a policeman? And wasn't he an honest man?

GORDA: I've got my hands on a lead. My lead's name is Leopold Lesca. Rich family. Licked the ass of the extreme right real good at a point when a certain big crook was in charge. But even the extreme right's too clean for him now. He's jumped in even deeper since. He's scraping off scum with his teeth even as we speak.

YVONNE: You're a low-life, that's all there is to it.

GORDA: I frequently think about how my father and all his friends struggled to insure that the century would turn out clean. (*Recalls an Italian workers' chant, breaks off in the middle, a pause, continues speaking.*) I waste my whole life hanging out in bars. The bed's empty and the woman who ought to be sleeping in it's gotten it into her head that there's something rotten in the state of Denmark.

LOULOU: What's Denmark got to do with it?

GORDA: (*Indicating* CLAUDIA.) That woman there, mark her well, is a queen!

CLAUDIA: Alright, who wants coffee?

SHE *exits without waiting for an answer.*

GORDA: Look at that power. Now that, that's real power! With a woman like that you could remake the world.

LOULOU: Put it another way, between you and her there's a fly or two in the ointment.

GORDA: I'm strong. I'm very strong. You're going to need me in the times ahead!

LOULOU: When the going gets rough, journalists get going.

CLAUDIA: (*Reentering with coffee.*) Go ahead, drink. That'll set you right up.

GORDA: Have you taken a good look at the big circus we've had around here lately? Have you? We're well on the way to total decomposition. Honest people invent little cautious words, by which they mean to say that it's really too bad, isn't it, but what can you do? And they wave their arms around like old trash, with a weak little apologetic smile, and they turn around and walk back into their store and vote the way they've always voted—for people who shake their hands and smile at them, and who talk a bunch of crap, and who deep down in their soul, despise them. Citizens of all lands, awake!

YVONNE: Tell him to cut it out.

GORDA: And meanwhile idiocy, evil, is creeping up on us, growing. It's going to slip inside us all before long! All it'll take is a whistle and boom, they'll re-light the ovens! Get the trains moving again! Come on! Stoke the engine, Yvonne, stoke it!

YVONNE: They may have killed some people back then, it's true, but at least they didn't use such foul language all the time.

GORDA: One day they'll have my hide.

LOULOU: Who's after you?

CLAUDIA: This morning, someone left a package in front of our door. A cat with its throat cut, slit from the chin right down to its tail

YVONNE: My God, how awful!

CLAUDIA: It's because of his articles on the assassination attempts.

GORDA: Name's Gianni Gorda! Journalist-tightrope-ist, high wire-ist! Often dream that the hearse is passing by and inside, my own esteemed cadaver. The crowning glory of journalism! A funeral wreath from the Socialist Party—"To our comrade Gianni, who died for his ideals," or else "Fascism will not survive," or else "Democracy is as dark as the grave." And at the foot of the tall trees, all the guard dogs can be heard barking. There are murders aplenty, but no guilty parties are found. We're all in the shit up to here. If you touch pitch, you come up covered in shit.

CLAUDIA: Okay, you've said what you had to say. That'll be quite enough now.

YVONNE: And that's the kind of husband you want? You've grown up all crooked. No one wants to believe in anything anymore. You wind up feeling like an empty jar. (*To* GORDA.) You've stuffed her head full of all your political crap. You're the one! You! Before she was pure. She was my little girl. Now she doesn't even recognize her own mother anymore! Thanks to you!

GORDA: I'm going to smash your face in.

YVONNE: Thief! Wop!

GORDA: I'm not staying here one more second.

HE *exits*.

CLAUDIA: I had a present for you.

YVONNE: Why don't you give it to some Arab instead.

LOULOU: Pretty nice party!

## SCENE SIX

CLAUDIA *is now in the street. She bumps into* FREDDY, *and her car keys drop.* FREDDY *picks them up.*

FREDDY: Hey! Where ya headin'?

CLAUDIA: What's it to you?

FREDDY: In a big rush?

CLAUDIA: Alright, give me back my keys.

FREDDY: Scared, are ya?

CLAUDIA: Scared? Me, scared?

FREDDY: 's normal. Pussy. Don't know me, so you're scared.

CLAUDIA: Of what, I wonder?

FREDDY: Rape of course.

CLAUDIA: Rape. Just try it and see how far you get.

FREDDY: Easy. I'm a chauffeur, 'm waiting for my boss, and you happen to pass by. Why, son of a bitch, a little orphan child, I say to myself, let's walk over and have a nice little chat. An ass lying on velvet's a comfortable way to have a chat, heats up the conversation in no time.

CLAUDIA: I have nothing to say to you.

FREDDY: Is it a crime to open a conversation with somebody? Even if you don't know them. Even if it's just to suggest a little hop in the hay in between two blank spots? Here I am. Why not make the most of it? Into the saddle! Off for a gallop. You ever think about the biggest champion bicycle racers? Know Fausto Coppi? Eddy Merckx, Bernard Hinault? Know 'em? And have you ever stopped to think what the difference is between them and all the second-raters? It ain't how strong their calves are little lady. It's the brain! The brain! The mental! Real C.E.O.'s, leaders of men, bosses for Christ's sake. So when you get into your car you know where you're going and who you're driving for. It's only logical! Oh sure, sure sure sure, there's people who take dope, yes, fine, fine, okay, people take dope. People take dope, and I'm against it. But you never see the real big boys taking dope. You ever seen a big boy taking dope? Never! A big boy'll never take dope. The big boy gets over with his personality, makes it all click with his head. Politics, same deal! On the one hand a whole bunch of little dicks. On the other, a prick, a real big good giant prick. Now that one's the ace of spades. That man's one in a million. You turn your back on him for two minutes, and they'll make mincemeat out of you. Negroes? Ever see negroes? AIDS is gonna wipe 'em all out. What could be more obvious? They ain't capable of taking care of 'emselves. They don't understand the first thing about epidemics. They think they're getting theirs from some sorcerer. A guy can have a setback, but once he's taken a hit, he just has to hop back into the saddle and take off. That's my philosophy, boy! Not left, not right, don't even think about it, just go for the gold. Which is why bike racing to me's like holy wafer. You win, you lose, you compete. That's how I'd sum up existence.

CLAUDIA: Is that all? Are you quite done? Now, hand over the keys.

FREDDY: What keys?

CLAUDIA: Have you looked at me even for one second? At these eyes? The shape of my ears? The zit that's been on my chin since this morning? You know anything about the color of my soul? No! For you, I'm just a concept. . .

FREDDY: A concept? That's beat.

CLAUDIA: Yes, a concept. The woman you get your rocks off with, the ass you pat!

FREDDY: Yeah, well anyway, that's the most interesting thing about a woman.

CLAUDIA: And your brain, I know exactly what's inside of *it*! One thing for sure, I wouldn't want to take a tour inside. It couldn't be bird shit in there, 'cause bird shit at least brings good luck.

FREDDY: You trying to humiliate me? You are, ain't ya? You'd just love that.

CLAUDIA: You've figured it all out! Okay then, that's enough. I've wasted enough time here. The keys! The keys!

FREDDY: No way. Who the hell do you think you are, slut?

FREDDY *throws* HER *down onto the ground, gives* HER *a few kicks.* SHE *screams.* A MAN *enters.* HE *throws a kick at* FREDDY. THE LATTER *drops to his knees.*

FREDDY: I'm gonna clobber you!

MAN: Come on, let's get out of here.

CLAUDIA *and* THE MAN *rush off.* WILLY *and* CARMEN *enter, very elegantly dressed. Looking classy.*

WILLY: What's going on? You lose something?

FREDDY: I'll go get the car.

WILLY: Pig. You fucking pig. That woman there was running away. You tried to fuck her, didn't you? I can still see her ass in the whites of your eyes! I'm sure of it, you tried to fuck her. In the car, in my very own Mercedes. Alright! Great! A broad walks by, you feel frisky, you screw. Yeah, not bad. A horny guy's a horny guy, so say it! Don't look so ashamed. It's just nature we're talking about. But you better have the organ pointed high enough.

FREDDY: Ok, boss, that'll do.

WILLY: Do you have a way with women? I don't know. What's it take? The right touch? Or do you let 'em spit all over you? Not good at all.

CARMEN: It's not right. Is this car coming or not?

WILLY: It's coming, babe, it's coming!

CARMEN: All I mean is that a young woman like me has the right to certain consideration, especially if she smokes her cigarette elegantly as she's coming out of the movies and half the theatre's staring at her buttocks with desire. Freddy, the car please. You see, Willy, what I don't care for so much about with you, yes, yes, hear me out without getting pissed off. What I don't care for so much is the fact that your name is Willy. Because Willy and Carmen, no matter which way you turn it, it has a sound more like the street than like good manners. So I'm just wondering if it couldn't be changed. You see what I mean? Totally changed. I'm really wondering about that.

WILLY: Carmen, I'm going to give you the surprise of your life.

CARMEN: Say it anyway.

WILLY: Look at my hands. Touch them! You feel the scars? I had to do real shit work before I was even twenty years old. And then there was this rich old dame, and I hump her. And yeah, she liked it. When the lawyer opened up her will, you know what? There was something in there for me. I put it into a French-fry stand at the North Station. I reeked of cold cooking oil. As soon as I could, I bought me a respectable bar. Willy's place, the Patriot's Café. Now, in a manner of speaking, I travel in the highest circles. And a week ago those high circles sent me a sign. And I answered, okay, highest circles, okay, affirmative. So, hold onto your hat Carmen—I'm running for office! Willy DeWolf is running for political office!

CARMEN: You gotta go act like a clown in all the supermarkets? "Good day, miss, good day sir. Buying groceries, are you? How are you doing?"

WILLY: A Member of Parliament! Parliament! Willy DeWolf, a member of Parliament. Now, that's a bombshell! That's a blast! That's bells ringing! Bells bigger and louder than the church bells on Easter Sunday. You'll be a Member of Parliament's chick. How's that for dignity! We're heading straight for glory!

THEY *exit.* CLAUDIA *and* THE MAN *reenter.*

CLAUDIA: They all gone? He's not there? When he was standing in front of me, I felt strong like anything. Now I'm scared shitless.

MAN: You get used to it.

CLAUDIA: To fear? You get used to fear? I don't think so.

MAN: You feel bad?

CLAUDIA: Yeah, I feel like vomiting, but it'll pass.

MAN: Where I come from, fear makes us into excellent runners. We run real fast with our heads down. Sometimes you stop dead in your tracks on the sidewalk and never get up again.

CLAUDIA: Is there someone after you?

MAN: You know that guy?

CLAUDIA: What kind of work do you do?

MAN: I'm a writer.

CLAUDIA: And it's on account of what you write that you've got problems.

MAN: You could say that. The Almighty doesn't like competition, and those who serve the Almighty even less. But this state of affairs doesn't suit me. I have a voice. And I want it to be heard. But I could have been a shepherd in the country or an engineer in the city or a journalist or a waiter. The civil war wiped out all the special privileges: All throats were equal as far as the razor was concerned. And I had to act fast and hustle my particular throat off into a safe place.

CLAUDIA: They tried to kill you?

MAN: I don't feel like talking about it. You ought to go home. You want me to go with you? You'd better clean up that cut or it'll get infected.

CLAUDIA: Leaving your country's a privilege. Taking a plane's a privilege.

MAN: Yes.

CLAUDIA: And getting a visa is yet another privilege.

MAN: You're talking like a bird without a brain.

CLAUDIA: Why, because I say privilege?

MAN: You don't have the right to talk like that.

CLAUDIA: Isn't it a privilege to have a choice? There are people in the world without any choices. They're in one place, and there they stay. No way to move. No way to get out. No plane and no passport.

MAN: Should I have died maybe? And when I was dead would I have had the right to your sympathy? Why is it that I hang on to life? I disappoint your sense of heroism maybe? Because I'm not a martyr? I don't elicit pity? Oh, I'm so sorry!!! What must you think of me? That I'm some kind of rat hiding out in the middle of your country? Oh, I'm so lucky, aren't I? I get to be treated like a piece of shit by your fellow citizens. Without any papers, any family, doing physical labor illegally on building sites, great! And I'm in good health, which is pretty annoying right there! I have two scars too. A knife slash in the thorax, another in the back. Want to see my scars? I'll show them to you. Would that raise me in your esteem?

CLAUDIA: I didn't mean to hurt you.

MAN: You have hurt me. (SHE *goes off.*) Don't leave. Stay. Please.

CLAUDIA: Do you have any idea of what's going on around here these days?

MAN: The assassination attempts?

CLAUDIA: I often ask myself exactly what kind of courage is needed to stand up and fight against it. What does it really mean to go all the way? To go all the way. Get yourself killed? Kill someone else? Murder in cold blood? Wholesale massacre? Give me one good reason why those people shouldn't be wiped out?

MAN: People who fight lose their humanity. They lose it even if the cause is just. That's what I see in your eyes. Your eyes are telling me something like that. But maybe you don't want me to talk about it? It hits me at night. I wake up in a cold sweat. The teeth of my dead friends are scraping the wood off their coffins. You can hear their bones rattling against the boards. And a voice with no face too. The voice says: Death to whoever causes death. So, there I am, sitting on the bed sweating. And in my mind I grab the razor and slit my enemies' throats. In the sheets, the smell of blood? Yes, yes! Even dying men, I slit their throats. Making an enemy croak twice over isn't going too far. And then I get up and I write. And I write and I write. The urge weakens, and I'm a little ashamed. I rub up against sentences, warm myself on them. I tranquilize myself with them. You see, I'm a man of privilege: I build myself a rocket, and I fly off on it whenever I feel like. You're still trembling. You're not scared on account of that guy. Your fear's something else. It's hate. You hated that guy just now. With all your might. You could have bitten his dick off. You could have killed him. You would have taken pleasure in it. Is that what horrifies you? The cruelty? The blood pumping into your mouth? That you're capable of going so far? You? Vengeance! It makes you choke! It makes you come. We're potential executioners. You and me both. It's taken me a long time to admit that I'm a potential executioner. Now that I know it, I'm less scared. I look around me. Each man possesses a dangerous boundary. On the other side of that boundary there's a demon, and if you don't say no to that demon, you become less of a man. We've got to say it over and over to ourselves.

CLAUDIA: That's just what I do. Every day, and every minute of every day!

MAN: Now, I've got to leave you. What's your name?

CLAUDIA: Claudia.

MAN: Goodbye, Claudia. I'm glad I could help you out.

CLAUDIA: Wait! I don't want to be alone tonight. Stay with me.

MAN: Back where I come from, there's a woman. She's on the terrace of our house. I'd like to be able to be back there with her. I'd like to hold her close in my arms. I love her.

CLAUDIA: It'll be one night. One night only. Just this one, and after we'll both go our separate ways. Coming along?

## PART TWO

### SCENE ONE

*Several months later. Newspaper headquarters.*

MINISTER OF THE INTERIOR: (*To* GIANNI GORDA, *with* CLAUDIA *there also.*) This cigarette lighter. I was standing right under the chandelier in your living room when I put it into your father's hand. It was snowing. It was December. "Merry Christmas, Pietro." And boom, tears. That's right. "I'm not a kid anymore, you know," he goes. And yet in a way he was. Not because of the cigarette lighter of course, but rather because he never saw the world with the eyes of a real adult. Your father was outraged by everything. He saw injustice everywhere. One image haunted him: It was Nietzsche in Torino, Nietzsche slipping into insanity! Nietzsche running to the rescue of an old horse being mistreated by a coachman! After that, there wasn't an injustice in the world that could take place without your father yelling at me: Nietzsche's horse! Nietzsche's horse! And I answered that there was nothing I could do about it. I'm just one tiny little man of politics, old man—a rank beginner, a novice. There's nothing I can do about it. It's beyond us. It sweeps over us like a raging wind. We're tossed about like walnut shells on an ocean deep at night in the middle of spring tide. And he answered, with a hard note in his voice—You're a sly one. You'll be a minister one day. And he was right. I'm minister of the interior. But when it comes right down to it, what am I actually able to do? Not a whole hell of a lot. A minister has to do other peoples' bidding. More than you'd imagine. Do you know that you resemble your father a great deal? The same silent, secret bull-headedness. You know, you can often find a will of iron and an inability to see together in the same person. With every bone in his body, he wants something and he doesn't even know what. That's what it means to be human. Are you so sure you don't relish the whips and scorns of outrageous fortune? To an extreme, like your father? I bet in fact that more than anything you love getting yourself into big messes? That you just love wallowing in pigsties? I can't help but wonder.

*Silence.*

You know the expression, a pyrrhic victory? You call something a pyrrhic victory when the victory costs more than the defeat. All idealists like to have pyrrhic victories, don't you agree? No matter what the after-effects are, it's the principle that counts for them. Victory, in principle. That Leopold Lesca of yours is a nutcase! For your information we're fully aware of it. We've got photos of him, framed photos. And we're starting to form a pretty good idea of the nature of the armed force that's backing him up. Now, that's the important part. But that, that particular information—absolutely explosive!!!—is that something we should shove in the face of the regular guy sitting in front of his T.V. set at eight o'clock at night? We'll handle this business alright, but in our own way, quietly, discreetly. Every time you bring facts to that regular guy's attention, facts which shatter his faith in the people entrusted to guard our institutions, you weaken democracy. You deepen the furrow of denigration. All dictatorships whose hands are dripping red deepen the furrow of denigration. And that's when they start to say, "The politicians are good for nothing. Where can we find that one providential man, that leader? Where's the clean sweep, the authoritarian personality, the mighty fist!? For a limited time only, rest assured, just long enough to put the train back on track." It's the same old refrain of denigration that keeps us here on this downhill slide we're on!!!

*Silence.*

At this very moment, you're asking yourself if I'm not the devil incarnate, aren't you? Or you might even be dying to spit in my face. Or at the very least, you're thinking, "Lesca's just a mongrel, a kind of foot soldier. But that politician, what's going on with him?" That big fat guy with his face full of purple veins, his high blood pressure, his cholesterol, his prostate, what's the real story there? Just another mercenary waving his lily white hands around? Just another rich guy who holds his constituency in utter contempt? An expert at I didn't know anything about it, at I had no idea, at the whole thing was going on behind my back? I am what I am. All of the above, which is just another way of saying: a realist? Yes. And a skillful negotiator? Yes. But I also happen to be standing alongside another man at the moment, a man I think of as my very own son.

*Silence.*

You owe me a lot. I make that statement in all seriousness, without the slightest arrogance. I'm not talking about your professional life: That you did without my help. Or practically. I'm talking about a more fundamental debt. A debt almost in the philosophical sense of the term. But regardless, a real debt: The kind of debt a young man contracts from an older man when he comes to him one day and puts his life in his hands, asking him to give him one good reason to exist. Do you remember that day? Give me one good reason to exist. You needed me then!!! A chasm had opened up at your feet. That, according to general usage, is what's known as life. You needed me!!! Me. Not your father. You didn't need his buckets of indignant tears. Was his indignation enough for you? No. You needed a man from a different world, a listener with his feet on the ground, the kind of man that you a priori don't generally like. I was there. I said: Present and accounted for!!! I said, don't flinch. Sign a pact with what's possible. Turn yourself into a useful man. And you set right in militating. Didn't you become useful? Hasn't the field of possibilities widened considerably for you? Have you forgotten that? I come here today to get you to renew that pact. Keep what you know to yourself. Do not succumb to the temptation to make yourself into a hero. Turn away from that romantic image of yourself as a supreme court judge. Stop thinking about your father! Think of me!!!

MINISTER OF INTERIOR *exits.*

CLAUDIA: What are you going to do?

GORDA: Keep going. Right to the finish.

CLAUDIA: Yes! Alright, then. I'll go down to the photo archives.

SHE *exits.* GORDA *starts to reread his article.*

GORDA: "A new attack on a supermarket and the premeditated murder of ten people yesterday has catapulted the pack of assassins onto everyone's front burner. An ever-increasing number of voices are being raised to denounce the inertia of the representatives of the law. And once again the question is raised of possible collusion between the extreme right and certain individuals belonging to the police force. When he was questioned on this subject, the Minister of Interior conceded that an inquiry was in progress, but that it would be several months before any conclusions were reached. The clues pile up, the trails intersect, but for those in charge, these issues seem not to be high on their list of priorities. Preoccupied with the impending elections, the members of the government prefer to stick their heads in the sand. Their chief priority seems to be to do nothing. How many victims do there have to be before our democracy in the best sense of the word gives the jump-start necessary to eliminate the bad policies which drive the nation?"

JULIAN *enters. He is soon joined by* LEOPOLD LESCA.

JULIAN: I'm looking for Gianni Gorda. Is he here?

GORDA: Why do you ask?

LESCA: Mr. Reporter! I'm Leopold Lesca. Perhaps you recognize me.

GORDA: What do you want?

LESCA: I read your articles on a daily basis. I'm not at all pleased with you. So, I said to myself, I'll just go right over to the Place de Louvain, and give that scalawag a piece of my mind!

GORDA: Kindly leave, sir.

LESCA: I'm amazed. You're older than I imagined. When I read your stuff, I pictured you as a young enthusiast, an eager beaver who gets all worked up lighting matches. Beware, I said to myself, he'd better beware, for he's forgotten the conventional wisdom: He who sows the wind, reaps the whirlwind.

GORDA: A warning?

LESCA: Let's not jump to such dire conclusions.

GORDA: I'm just doing my job.

LESCA: Good Heavens, of course you are. See that, Julian, he's doing his job. For certain people, work consists of saying false things about good people.

JULIAN: What does he want anyway?

LESCA: I think he sees me mixed up in some mysterious conspiracy.

JULIAN: What conspiracy?

LESCA: How should I know?

GORDA: Everyone knows you're a low-life, that you're a swindler, a cheat, a fraud, a megalomaniac, and that you've dirtied your hands through dealings in shady money.

LESCA: Slander, Julian. Do you hear the sound of slander in the air?

GORDA: The list of achievements doesn't stop there. I'm going to prove it. I have names on this piece of paper. Read them and tell if you don't know these persons.

LESCA: Nope, don't know them.

GORDA: Are you sure?

LESCA: Hundred percent sure.

GORDA: Some of them you met quite recently. What were you doing Saturday, the 23rd of last month?

LESCA: We were right to come here. This is getting exciting! The 23rd? The 23rd? Good question, that! Alright. I've brought along a leading man who's going to answer for me.

JULIAN: Me, sir?

LESCA: Yeah, sure, Julian, the 23rd, for God's sake. It's a date! You can't forget dates like that. One date, Julian, one lousy date. A goddamn fucking date! What were we doing on the 23rd, come on!

JULIAN: I don't know, sir.

LESCA: Concentrate, concentrate on the 23rd. The 23rd. The 23rd. The 23rd.

JULIAN: You're making fun of me! What am I supposed to say?

LESCA: The whole truth and nothing but the truth, obviously!

JULIAN: Well, shit, I don't remember! We were talking.

LESCA: There we go! We were talking!

JULIAN: You gave me some books. We were discussing some...

LESCA: Discussing some! Discussing some! There, there you have it! Are you happy now, Inspector Clouseau? No, Inspector Clouseau's not happy. Deposition by Leopold Lesca, this day, before the press. Saturday the 23rd, woke up at dawn, and wrapped in the aroma of piping hot coffee, he spoke at length with his young friend here. A rather brilliant conversation, I must admit, on the subject of regeneration. Go ahead.

Take out all the tools of your trade: Note pad, pencil, and write away! Julian confessed to all the doubts he had, not on the idea of regeneration as such, but regarding the fashion, tragic to say the least, in which it has manifested in the first half of our young century. We had a good laugh, didn't we? I put two of my fingers under my nose and I said to him, "Hey Julian, would you mistake me for Hitler?" Do I look like some kind of skinhead looking backward into the past? Do you really think that the person standing here is some kind of relic carving swastikas on the trees that stand on his property? Julian understood me. He truly saw that I'm a new man because I throw myself wholeheartedly into the arms of contemporary life. There are a few elementary principles in life as we know it. There's order and disorder. There's the high and the low. There are those who are high up and those who are down below, and the snake of equality is one smartass devouring his own tail. Do I look like I live a complicated life, or like I've got complicated ideas? You shouldn't waste your time on me. I'm the wrong guy. Contact with me can only lead to disappointments and even setbacks.

CLAUDIA *enters.*

CLAUDIA: There aren't any good photos of the victims, just a negative. . .

LESCA: What do you know, the Most Blessed Virgin!

CLAUDIA: What's he doing here?

LESCA: You've got a remarkably big mouth. What a big mouth you have! A big mouth can come in handy for a woman. (*To* JULIAN.) The lady is the gentleman's chick. And also his secretary. That's nice. It's admirable. Couples who work together. We're going to let you get back to your work. We've already gone. Don't show us out. Madam, my compliments. Nice little skit we all put on, hm? Pretty funny, and with such limited scenery too.

CLAUDIA: Out, out, out, out!

LESCA: What eyes! What eyes she has! Did you see them? With eyes like that she could kill a buffalo!

THEY *exit.*

GORDA: That guy's fucking outrageous!

CLAUDIA: I hope you're not telling me you admire the guy.

GORDA: Claudia, let's not start in again!

CLAUDIA: You think he's impressive, don't you?

GORDA: Come over here by me.

SHE *goes farther off.*

CLAUDIA: As far as photos go, there's very little usable material. Except maybe these here. Have a look. (*A new attempt at a reconciliation.*)

GORDA: The world's out of whack. But that's no reason for me not to touch you.

CLAUDIA: Yes, it happens to be an excellent reason! I have a hard time getting myself clean every day, using soap and water. I draw blood each time because I scratch myself so hard with my nails, and yet that odor is there, the smell of shame. And you, what do you do? Nothing. You do nothing for me. You don't do a thing. You just let me hang there like a dead branch.

GORDA: I kiss you, I take you in my arms.

CLAUDIA: And that makes me deliriously happy, and a feeling of pleasure runs through my whole body. It borders on violence, and I start to forget my own name. At that moment, I don't care if things turn out for better or worse. And that, that's what I absolutely refuse to have happen anymore. Lesca's got to be destroyed. Now. This instant. Destroy him. If you accept that man for an instant, for one single instant, for a fraction of a second even, the way he is, then what does that make you? Him, obviously! Him! Him! You turn into him, without any further ado! You're finished! What he does, you're doing, and what he wants you to do, that you do too. Charisma is filthy. Charisma's disgusting. Charisma's a sticky substance that seeps inside you when you're not looking, and after that you simply stride merrily straight toward the wrong aim. They stick your head in a sack and your brains start to stink since they're rotting from disuse!

GORDA: Calm down.

CLAUDIA: Fuck calm!

GORDA: Some coffee?

CLAUDIA: I'm ashamed of myself. Ashamed! Ashamed of the way we're all so cynical.

GORDA: I'm doing all I can about Lesca.

HE *holds out his article to her.* SHE *skims through it rapidly.*

CLAUDIA: No names, of course. The names are all for Claudia at four in the morning when she's crying in the john because she's been waiting for hours already and the night's getting darker and darker, and you haven't come back. But the next day, we're all so calm and serene, names in the paper a thing of the past. Not one single name. But narratives yes, plenty of narratives with a coefficient of probability.

GORDA: I'm gathering together the proof. Every proof there is. And once I've got them all, we'll print the names.

CLAUDIA: How?

GORDA: An informer. I'd prefer to say no more than that.

CLAUDIA: If it keeps on this way, I won't be able to love anybody anymore. Last night, my mother called. Gallons of tears, and all because a woman's body doesn't last forever! She was talking, crying, and all of a sudden a voice rose up in me—don't give in to fear, the voice said. I couldn't make it stop. Don't give in to fear. One day your mother's fear will be your own fear, and you'll be scared, same as her. I don't want that to happen to me. I don't want it!

GORDA: (*Pointing to a photo.*) What do you think of that one? The contrast's better, no?

CLAUDIA: You're not listening to me.

GORDA: You're talking a lot louder than you think.

CLAUDIA: You don't listen to me and then you go off spouting drivel.

GORDA: I'm just trying to finish this article.

CLAUDIA: Following that last time we saw my mother, I bumped into some boy in the street, and I slept with him. That's why I didn't come home that night.

GORDA: I had a feeling, believe it or not!

CLAUDIA: I'm not sorry.

GORDA: Who's asking you to be?

CLAUDIA: I wasn't trying to get back at you.

GORDA: Nobody's throwing you out. Not me, that's for sure. Every day, I say to myself that the charm's kind of shaky, but it's still working. The charm's been working this long. I don't want you to leave. Tonight, while I was walking around town, I thought of you: she's expecting a child. I hope it has her face, a gorgeous fiery face.

CLAUDIA: Do you think that one day I'll have enough courage to wait for a Lesca on his doorstep and sink two bullets in his head?

GORDA: He'll pay. I promise you, he'll pay.

CLAUDIA: No rest for his ashes, no rest for his wicked ashes!

GORDA: You're magnificent.

CLAUDIA: Stop! I could never keep loving a man who was that blind!

GORDA: All I said was that I wanted to kiss you.

CLAUDIA: Well do it. Do it for Christ's sake. What are you waiting for? (HE *does it.*)

## SCENE TWO

*In the Patriot's Café,* CARMEN *is alone in the dark.* SHE *is waiting, bored. Sounds can be heard coming from the café, especially* YVONNE*'s voice.*

YVONNE: Carmen? Carmen?

*No answer. The door opens. Enter* YVONNE. *She is surprised to see* CARMEN *sitting there in the dark.*

YVONNE: What are you doing?

CARMEN: I'm looking at the sky.

YVONNE: In the dark? With your eyes closed?

CARMEN: It's most beautiful that way.

YVONNE: I need a hand. Can you come down?

CARMEN: I can't. My nails are still wet.

YVONNE: You're pathetic!

YVONNE *exits, furious.* CARMEN *stays there in the dark. All of a sudden, the lights come on. Enter* FREDDY. *It can now be seen that* CARMEN *is wearing a wig which changes the cut and color of her hair, a pull-over, and jeans.*

FREDDY: The boss sent me.

CARMEN: It's about time! Two hours I've been waiting.

FREDDY: (*Pointing at her get-up.*) What the hell's all that? Willy won't like it. He said he wanted you to go the extra mile, that he wanted you to show up looking classy, real classy. That "you ain't going out to eat with low-lives" on his thirty-first birthday.

CARMEN: This is what I put on. It's the way I like it.

FREDDY: And then he said, "That woman's a princess. She's got clouds floating around her head. She talks like an angel. You look after her every second of every day. Whatever she asks for, you do it. If she asks you to uncork twelve bottles of champagne, you do it. Don't haggle, don't try to trick her out of it, just do it. So, you gotta be like a dog. Love her like a dog. Lick her ankle with that nice, fat bulldog tongue of yours."

CARMEN: Willy's so nice.

FREDDY: So you're the mistress and I'm the dog.

CARMEN: So?

FREDDY: So the equation couldn't be simpler: either we do it or we don't do it.

CARMEN: Do what?

FREDDY: I'm hung like a gorilla. I only mention it 'cause it's true. I've had 'em all: secretaries, bank tellers, office-clerks. Travel agent, nurse, cleaning lady. Had me some that made me sweat, some as crazy as they can get, some Paulettes and one or two Juliettes, but, believe it or not, I ain't never had no Carmen!

CARMEN: Get back, baboon.

FREDDY: Kiss, then open wide.

CARMEN: I just have to see that face in my mind's eye, that beefy, macho face of yours and I lose interest.

FREDDY: I can do ya the soapy saucepan. Lick the baron. The cone with two scoops? You choose! Little Josie and her three houses, know that one? That's my specialty, little Josie and her three houses!

CARMEN: A person's gotta have a damn good reason before she does stuff. Something special! You, you're just a mass of habits. You even screw out of habit. You're nothing but a machine that runs on automatic pilot.

FREDDY: Little bitch!

CARMEN: You're a total loss, Freddy, and you don't even know it.

FREDDY: You're in my head at night. I put your knees over your shoulders, your triangle, I open you up with my tongue, and then you howl 'cause I know how to wriggle my tongue like nobody's business.

CARMEN: Thank you my good man. Just leave your address at the door and we'll be calling you.

FREDDY: (*Rapping.*) When I starts getting hot, gotta stick the old wiener in a pot.

CARMEN: Why don't you just stick it under the faucet? You'll get over it. Go on, clear out of here.

FREDDY: I've had enough standing around waiting in the wings. I've had it with cleaning up other peoples' crud. I may come from the gutter, but I got wings, baby. I'm a golf pro, a swinger. Come on, let's get down now!

CARMEN: I'm never getting down with you.

FREDDY: On the sexy side of things, you do okay, but on the brain side, there's a screw loose somewhere. 'Cause if I ever mentioned to Willy about that florist philosopher I saw you with in that bar, his feathers might get ruffled, if you see what I mean.

CARMEN: You poor sap!

FREDDY: Who are you to talk to me like that? A whore. Nothing but a whore.

CARMEN: I am not a whore. There's a price attached to my services, and what I get I pay for. When it comes to the world of money, that's the only honest way to operate. Don't you dare call me a whore. I made a deal for myself 'cause it was the only choice I had. That shit-for-brains little head of yours can't grasp that. Don't you ever come near me, and don't you ever lay a hand on me.

FREDDY: The day'll come when you'll suck my toes.

*Telephone.*

CARMEN: Willy? Yeah, yeah, we're coming. No, it's Freddy. He's telling me all about his toes. Yeah, yeah, I'll let him know. We'll be right there.

FREDDY: You gonna keep your mouth shut? You gonna tell him?

CARMEN: How about you, what are you gonna say?

FREDDY: I was just kidding around.

CARMEN: Give me the keys. I'm driving.

## SCENE THREE

*Sidewalk café. The rank and file of the Extreme Right have all converged inside.* LESCA *comes outside the restaurant to smoke a cigarette.*

GUEST 1: What do you think of that?

LESCA: Dreadful. The western world is sinking in quicksand, that's the heart of the matter. But the combat must proceed within legal boundaries!!! Imbeciles! Cowards! Mediocrity! Where is the heroism we're looking for? Where's the thrill of adventure?

ANOTHER DINNER GUEST *comes out to join* THEM.

GUEST 2: The falsified documents? The passport? Everything ready?

GUEST 1: All set. Our contacts on the police force took care of the whole thing.

GUEST 2: Has anyone notified our friends in Austria?

GUEST 1: Yes, I told them as little as possible. That we're sending them someone important. And that they'll have to take it from there. That's all.

GUEST 2: Fine.

LESCA: I'm not going to go.

GUEST 2: That's not smart!

LESCA: Calm down. Don't you believe in patron saints?

GUEST 2: It's not going to work. You're playing with fire. It's the classic set-up. There's no way around it this time. They know all about our business, and they'll get you on racketeering. They'll dig down deep and come back up with the rest of us.

LESCA: He's just a windbag, that reporter.

GUEST 2: Does that kid really have the goods?

LESCA: He knows nothing.

GUEST 1: Pull yourself together! That little scumbag's got him all hot and bothered.

LESCA: One more remark like that out of you, and I'll smash your face in.

GUEST 1: And will you assume responsibility for the consequences? Are you aware of what's involved?

LESCA: My dear prosecutor, I like you. But like all frightened people, you move forward at a snail's pace. Let's all calm down. Is there truly any reason to fly into a panic? None. So I'm staying put.

WILLY *leaves the table inside and joins* THE OTHERS *outside*.

LESCA: (*Provocatively, aggressive.*) So DeWolf, your election campaign going great guns?

WILLY: Yesterday I had my best rally yet. I was brilliant.

LESCA: Brilliant!

WILLY: I had that audience in the palm of my hand, I could feel it! I went at them something like this: "I'm not a politician. I'm a man, pure and simple. I'm scared of dying. I like a good meal. I like women. I speak right from my belly, that's where my power lies! In my belly! My guts! If I've got something in my head, it passes through yards and yards of innards first. And believe you me, I think more clearly than all those guys who fart it out the tops of their heads. You know what I like? I like the guy who comes up to the counter of my bar and tells me: 'Willy, I feel good here, it's like a home to me here.' And then I treat him to a drink. And while he's knocking it back, I look past his shoulder and I ask myself what's going on out there? And I see people out in the street just hanging out, who ought to be somewhere else, like maybe getting a nice tan on the sand for example. And then I treat my customer to another drink, and toast his health. And you know what I'd like? For my daughter to be able to walk down the street with her girlfriend without having to be called a whore. It's very simple. It's downright basic. Is there anyone here, man or woman, who likes it when their daughter's called a whore? Who? Let's see some hands."

LESCA: (*Cutting him off.*) And what I generally say is: In our party there lot's of talk, but precious little action.

WILLY: Are you saying that for my benefit?

LESCA: Oh no! Not at all! My dear friend, how could you imagine a thing like that? You're not the issue, not in the slightest. This is the first time we're even meeting, isn't it? Well, the first time we've ever spoken together anyway.

WILLY: You don't come to my bar, that's for sure!

LESCA: I don't like bars. You run into all sorts of riff-raff there. I'd rather have a few friends over to my house. At this moment I've one staying with me who I like a lot. In a funny way, it's he who brought us together, what do you say to that? Carmen? Does that ring any bells—Carmen? Well, he's got it into his head that this Carmen of yours is the whole reason for his existence. He talks about her. He gives details. A whole lot of details. Details about body hair, for example! I've had to rearrange some of his thinking. It should all work out in the end. Love fades. But the patient is still shaky on his feet. I even think it possible that the little bugger could have a relapse, if you see what I mean. Oh, yes! Let's suppose that Carmen shows up again. An old heart-throb, well, you can't wait to see her, isn't that right? Frailty, thy name is woman! What I mean, dear sir, is that it would be personally distasteful to me to see my young friend harassed by hysterical phone calls. I beg your pardon. I'm sure this is all a tempest in a teapot and that I'm giving you the impression of being discourteous. I'm so sorry, *mein Herr*! In the matter at hand, I'm afraid we're in bed together, if I may be so bold. (HE *sticks two fingers up on his head, in the form of horns.*) You follow? We have the same interests at heart. You still follow? So, lay down the law, my friend. Vigilance, vigilance. This is no time to loosen the reins on your fairy princess! If I may say so.

CARMEN *appears.*

CARMEN: Willy, I'm here!

LESCA: Ah, here's your chick! Cheerio, DeWolf. It's been a great pleasure. Don't forget. It wouldn't do for there to be a public scandal! The Carmens of the world are forever sniffing at the toreadors. (HE *goes out singing the "Toreador Song" from* Carmen.)

GUEST 1: Has he totally lost it?

GUEST 2: This business will be death of us!

*Exit* LESCA *and* HIS FRIENDS. LESCA *comes back.*

LESCA: (*Still provocative.*) Keep your eye peeled. Just between us, I wouldn't like her showing up at my house and giving him a private viewing of her panties!

LESCA *exits.*

WILLY: Dirty bastard! Worm!

CARMEN: What did that guy want?

WILLY: Nothing. Let's go home.

CARMEN: Oh, no baby! I came for the dessert and I'm eating it.

WILLY: Okay, okay, fine, that's alright. You do just what you want. You eat all the dessert you want!!!

## SCENE FOUR

*A street. The banquet is over.* CARMEN *and* WILLY *are walking back to their car.* WILLY, *standing, drunk as a tree about to fall.*

WILLY: Leopold Lesca. Faggot! He talks to me, and it's just like someone putting his foot down on a piece of shit. "My dear DeWolf, what a superb spread! Fine cuisine calls for real connoisseurs." One day I'm gonna say something to the president: I respect your opinions, chief, but I ain't gonna belong to no party that cozies up to nellies.

HE *lets out a giant belch, then starts to feel nauseous.*

CARMEN: Listen, if you need to drink, drink! But it's kind of disgusting having you vomit on my feet. And don't think for a minute that I'm gonna waste one second of my time carrying you home. That's just bullshit!

WILLY: Member of Parliament Willy DeWolf! If I get elected all the toilets'll be made out of marble.

CARMEN: Which won't stop you from missing the bowl, hunh!

WILLY: All the patriots will shit in marble!

WILLY *tries to walk, but falls down onto his backside.*

CARMEN: Can you at least make an effort just to get to the car?

SHE *tries to hoist him back up.* SHE *hasn't spotted* JULIAN, *who seems to have gotten his act together and is almost unrecognizable.* HE *has been staring at* HER *since the beginning of the scene.*

JULIAN: A sandbag's hard to lift. You won't be able to handle it.

CARMEN: Who's that talking? I know that voice. Julian! It's Julian.

JULIAN: All dressed up!

CARMEN: It's my Julian.

JULIAN: You smell like you've been packing it away.

CARMEN: My breath may have a faint whiff of wine, but I'm not drunk.

JULIAN: Don't go to any trouble on my account, Carmen.

CARMEN: Why did you come here? Just for the show? A little call-girl, that's all I am, right? It wasn't worth coming outside for something so petty, Julian. Did it serve any real purpose? I'm just fine, if that's what you want to know. Because, what would we talk about now anyway? Back together like all the ex-lovers the world over. A porcelain dog, with nothing to say to each other. How's it going with you? Okay, and you? Yeah, things are alright. Yeah me too.

JULIAN: I've changed my ways. My eyes aren't red anymore.

CARMEN: Are you proud of yourself? You've become someone?

JULIAN: I struck oil.

CARMEN: How about money?

JULIAN: You want some? Here, take. I've got a new life in my pockets too.

CARMEN: You cozy up to the Pope or something? Sure looks like it.

JULIAN: Do you know what it means for a man to incarnate an idea? Such men really do exist. They send an electric current running right into your ear. It cuts right through the flab, and makes you hard, real hard. And the wire comes out your nose. And the world smiles at you like a new dawning.

CARMEN: You're totally whack, Julian. You caught some kind of disease?

JULIAN: I'm not the one who stinks of booze. (WILLY *comes to, scrambles to his feet.*)

WILLY: Who's the undertaker?

JULIAN: No one's talking to you.

WILLY: It's Refrigerator Man! Guy looks like a fucking ice floe. On your way, Captain Igloo, we don't dig the cold here. Watch out, babe, watch out for freeze-dried men passing in the night.

JULIAN: So that's who you screw with?

WILLY: Who told you you could talk to this woman? By what right? Oh, it's the florist! Now I see. It's the florist. That faggot's little buddy. The tulip salesman. Go ahead, set up your flower stands. If it's the wind blew you this way, then it's an ill wind. And it's gonna stink up the whole neighborhood. A cipher doesn't address a goddess. No, he's got a bitter taste in his mouth, and it's crammed full of dead leaves. And as for his balls, them he keeps nice and snug, tucked inside his pants.

JULIAN: Well I must say, that's very nicely put! Do you, by any chance, put your cigarette butts out in your gravy, sir?

WILLY: Listen, McDork, each and every intellectual is gonna die from brain-rot. Won't that be poetic justice? Alright already, this is starting to get tired. Okay, I pull and you, you just follow me and keep it shut.

CARMEN: Are you talking to your dog? No? I thought you were.

WILLY: Ease up, slut.

CARMEN: Only a shithead would talk like that.

WILLY: Okay, okay. I just got a little hot under the collar. You don't have to nail me to the wall over it!

CARMEN: Big fat pig!

WILLY: What do you want me to do? Get down on my knees?

CARMEN: Have you taken a look at yourself lately, with that potbelly of yours, like some retired football player?

WILLY: Don't start in with me, Carmen? I'm not some twenty-pound weakling with ulcers lining his stomach! I give him just five minutes! After that, I mess him up good. Five minutes!

HE *goes off.*

CARMEN: Go fuck yourself!

JULIAN: It's about time!

CARMEN: You, beat it. I'm not looking for a best man for my wedding! And if it's cold outside, don't you worry your head about it, I know how to keep a roof over my head.

JULIAN: You look gray. Gray. Lousy.

CARMEN: You better not say that again.

JULIAN: It doesn't take very long for a person's soul to go bad. You don't seem to be aware of that.

CARMEN: You little runt! If you had one ounce of tact, you'd have said, "Nobody has the right to judge that girl. She has secrets. Pigs can't see the enormous difference between what she looks like and who she really is, because pigs can't get into paradise!"

JULIAN: I'm ashamed of you. Ashamed of the love I have for you.

SHE *gives* HIM *a violent blow to the head.* HE *bleeds.*

CARMEN: There, that's for the shame.

SHE *rushes out. The crack of a thunderstorm is heard.*

## SCENE FIVE

*Yvonne's. The storm can still be heard coming down.* CARMEN *has just come in. Soaking wet.* CLAUDIA *is there.*

YVONNE: Life sure is something else! My God! The pains! The joys! I'm going to be a grandmother. Can you believe that? The girl just told me. That's what we've been needing around here. A baby! I find out I'm going to be a grandmother, and that's when you decide to come in with your eyes blazing with anger. My God! And what about poor Willy? Where is Willy now? Have you given him so much as a second thought? Maybe he couldn't find Freddy. Someone might have stolen his wallet. The streets are crawling with wolves!

CARMEN: Too bad on him.

YVONNE: You don't just leave a drunk man on the street all by himself!

CLAUDIA: Lay off of Carmen, okay?

YVONNE: A woman's made of equal parts of patience and suffering, and that's a lesson you haven't learned yet! Just look at the state you're in! You're soaking. Take your clothes off, and I'll go find you a nightgown. (YVONNE *exits.*)

CLAUDIA: What's that running down your face?

CARMEN: Rain!

CLAUDIA: Sure it isn't tears? Maybe you think you're the first person in the world who ever cried.

CARMEN: How about you, you cry a lot?

CLAUDIA: I cry, I laugh.

CARMEN: I'd give up my place in heaven to be a girl like you.

CLAUDIA: What's so special about me?

CARMEN: I don't know. Something that comes out of you. Something that warms a person like a fire on a cold day. I just know that your baby's going to have a beautiful square jaw, cut like with a chain-saw, and every one of his four sides standing straight and tall!

CLAUDIA: You're strong too! It shows in your eyes.

CARMEN: I'm just a machine. You put a token in the slot, and off it goes, gliding and chugging along!

CLAUDIA: What kind of thing is that to say!

CARMEN: I used to not give a shit. I let life roll over me, but what's the sense in that? All I can say is, there's a guy out there I love. I love, love, love, love. Why does a person have to have a war going on inside them all the time? If there's something you ain't got, you want it, and when you do got it, it turns out not to be what you wanted after all. Can you understand that?

YVONNE *reenters with the nightgown.*

YVONNE: Put that on.

GORDA: (*Offstage.*) Claudia?

GIANNI GORDA *enters.* HE *is holding a pile of newspapers in his hand.*

YVONNE: Oh, it's the alcoholic.

CLAUDIA: What's happening?

GORDA: Look. One less spook in the world. It'll never come between us in bed again.

CLAUDIA: Mom, look, the lie has a face!

YVONNE: What is it?

GORDA: I got Lesca. Background information, proofs, the works.

YVONNE: Filth and libel!

GORDA: Do you have any idea of what it was like in the editorial room an hour ago? Everyone, the whole staff from the secretary right up to the owner: "Yay, Gianni, congratulations, Gianni. Ya doin' okay, Gianni?" And Gianni Gorda was doing very okay. Gianni Gorda floated down the hallways, handsome and proud. Too bad my father wasn't there to see it. He'd have seen an incredibly calm look on my face. He would've been crying. He'd have said: "That boy's strong. He's proved himself worthy of his father." I got you, Lesca! I got you! What's a man who thinks he's indestructible? A midget! Yeah, a midget with one leg already poking out into the void. Poor Lesca, I really got him! You're going to have to open your eyes, Yvonne, because I'm not nobody. I'm a different person now. I weigh a thousand pounds lighter. Boy, it feels good to be so light! I feel like I'm right on the verge of doing great things. How come there's no champagne? Isn't this the right occasion? Don't I have the right to celebrate? What does it look like, the face of a guy who's been caught? Is he scared? He laughed at me! I'm sure he was laughing at me. He took me for a nut-case. Fuck you and your arrogance, Lesca! Fuck it! For once in your life, you're gonna smell squeaky clean! Claudia, I promise, we'll never mention his name again. Lesca, washed up, swept out, terminated, finished. All I'd really like is for someone to tell me that he's lying there in some corner with his face bashed in by the truth.

YVONNE: Out! Get out of my house, you. Out!

GORDA: Yes, I'm going, and I'll never set foot inside here again.

GORDA *exits*.

CLAUDIA: (*To* CARMEN.) Don't stay here. There's a bed waiting for you at our house.

CARMEN: What would I do at your house?

CLAUDIA: You're alone and you have a heart that's been drained dry. That doesn't do anyone any good. This whole country's twisted and we need every available hand to straighten it out!

CARMEN: What's all that got to do with me?

YVONNE: Now you're talking!

CLAUDIA: You sure you don't want to come? (CARMEN *shakes her head no.*) Well then, goodbye Carmen.

CARMEN: Goodbye, Claudia.

CLAUDIA *exits*.

YVONNE: Goodbye. (*Telephone rings.*) It's Willy!

CARMEN: You haven't seen me. Tell him I'm not here.

YVONNE: (*At the telephone.*) Hello? Yes. Yes. Don't worry yourself, Willy. She's here. Yes, yes, right here, next to me. She's fine. I think she's very, very sorry.

## SCENE SIX

LESCA, *at home.* HE *is reading the newspaper that contains* GORDA'*s article. Figuring out how to react. Lights up a cigarette. Picks up the telephone, dials a number.*

LESCA: It's Lesca. Let me talk to the public prosecutor. (*Holds.*) Not there? Fine. (*Dials another number.*) Is Bertrand there? Lesca. Fine. (*Dials another number, no answer.*) All absent.

*A voice in the shadows.*

JULIAN: I'm not.

LESCA *now notices* JULIAN *who has just walked in.*

LESCA: It's you. Come over here. Don't hang back there in the shadows.

JULIAN: Sir, they say. . . (HE *stops himself.*)

LESCA: They're saying what?

JULIAN: They're saying. . . (HE *stops himself.*)

LESCA: Are you talking about this?

HE *hands* HIM *the newspaper.*

JULIAN: Is it true?

LESCA: Everything is true.

JULIAN: No, it's not true! It's rot. Filth! You told me a million times that that paper was nothing but a dirty, filthy rag. And this proves it! That must be it.

You're testing me. Lies. Slander. None of it's true. It's all slander, isn't it? None of it's true, right? None of it.

LESCA: It's all true.

JULIAN: You're saying it was all true?

LESCA: Don't panic. The cause goes way beyond me. And it will keep going without me.

JULIAN: What's happening to me? I was dreaming. I got thrown from my bed. I stretched out my hand—it gets chopped to bits. I warmed myself against a man—it was a corpse. You're a corpse and you've got a corpse's hands and soul too.

LESCA: What are you going to do now?

JULIAN: This! (HE *spits in his face.*)

LESCA: Christ too suffered the weak to spit on him.

JULIAN: I admired you. I loved you. How could I be so gullible? It's humiliating!

LESCA: Weren't we bound together by a mutual virile desire? I loved that desire and I still do. I was not born of the same rain as you, the rain of tears, the rain of regrets, the water of repentance. I marched to the edge of the abyss like a brave man walks into a hail of bullets: With youth, with ardor, with pride. Knowing at every second that the precipice was there at my ankles. And even so, airborne, celestial as a warrior for the Grand Order must be. I'm not an assassin. More like a kind of priest. Does that astonish you? I bore the idea of sacrifice to new heights and lengths. I wanted to share it with you. Is that so hard to understand? When the finger presses down on the trigger, don't see it as a murder or an act of barbarism, only part of the long tradition of the strong and the weak, which causes our ancestors closed up in their tombs to smile. No, you don't understand. I can see quite clearly that you don't understand. You're nothing. A cipher. A joker. A deserter. In a very short time you'll be colorless as any democrat, eager for any transaction so long as they throw some coins in your face. (JULIAN *starts to leave.*) Wait! I'll give you one last chance. (HE *goes to get a weapon.*) This weapon is loaded. You're going to shoot me. That will be my ultimate message. Two bullets aimed exactly at my heart, by your hand. Remember what I taught you: Woe to the defeated!

JULIAN *raises the pistol, points it at* LESCA. *Just as* HE *presses down on the trigger,* HE *turns his arm away.*

JULIAN: I'm a failed student, master, a good-for-nothing, if I may say so.

LESCA: Fire! Fire! I order you to fire.

JULIAN: My dream's a dead dog. I'm not scared of you anymore. And I don't love you anymore. I've got another idea for what kind of finale we should have. Death is an uplifting reunion. Or that's what you've said so often. Now's the moment, lift me up!

LESCA: What do you want me to do?

JULIAN *tosses him the gun.*

JULIAN: Play me a tune on that. After all, you're the virtuoso, aren't you? (LESCA *points the gun at his jaw, hesitates a long time.*) Well, Maestro, got a cramp in your hand or what? What are you waiting for? Your finger still stiff?

LESCA: What pitiless irony from young Goret!

JULIAN: You sweating? Would you like to hear my theory on the subject? It's always easier if you've got a theory.

LESCA *raises the weapon, then lets it drop again.*

LESCA: I can't.

JULIAN: You can't.

LESCA: I can't.

JULIAN: We're going through some rough times, but just now, I'm especially happy with myself. I just taught you something: About a certain kind of cowardice that comes over a man when he's suddenly face to face with his own ideas. (*Police sirens.*) Ah, I leave you to the hands of justice and prison.

## SCENE SEVEN

*Patriot's Café.* A MAN *enters.* HE *walks with a cane, with difficulty.* LOULOU *greets the customer mechanically, paying no attention.*

LOULOU: Sir.

FLORKIN *looks at* HIM.

FLORKIN: Hello, my boy! Is that any way to talk to me? Don't you know who I am?

LOULOU: (*Delighted that he's here.*) Simon! Simon!

FLORKIN: So this is where I find you? Good God! This is where you are! I've been looking for you for weeks. Your grandmother told me you were here. But here where? We're not out in the countryside. It's the big city. "No, no, he hasn't come by to see me," I said. "That's how they are these days," she said. Why didn't you come to my house to see me? You don't like where I live? It's ugly? You didn't want to see me? That hurts. Why didn't you want to see me? So you're a waiter in a bar now? What's your boss like? It's DeWolf, that guy who's running for office. What's he really like? Does he at least treat you decently?

LOULOU: You'll see for yourself. In two minutes, he's going to be making a speech.

FLORKIN: I played my trumpet here. Just after the war. It was a bar back then too. That's where I first met Ginette and your grandmother. Did I ever tell you about Ginette? She wanted me to dance with her. I said no, I wouldn't. "Why," she asks? "It's on account of my feet." "What do you mean your feet?" They crushed them with the butts of their rifles. They arrest me, they deport me, I try to escape. The commandant of the camp says (*Imitating a German accent.*) "You're going to die anyway, but before you do, I'm going to teach you how to live. Take off your shoes. What pretty feet, dear friend, very pretty, even if they are disobedient." He takes a rifle, and. . . That's alright. He got the feet, but he didn't get the rest. The Americans got there. I was lucky. So Ginette gets really cuddly and says to me: "Simon, I'm the one who's going to make you forget your wounds." Incredible, no? I practically vomited with disgust at the idea of forgetting. Forgetting! With feet like these, she wanted me to forget six million Jews up in smoke! I cut off all contact. Never saw her again.

LOULOU: Yeah, that makes sense.

FLORKIN: I'm going to note down what your DeWolf has to say. I note down everything. I mix it all together and then I separate it according to subject. That's how I've gotten ahead in life. I taught myself everything! No school. You can ask anyone for Simon Florkin in my neighborhood, and they'll say, "Oh yes, the autodidact!" Well, who knows what the word means anyway.

LOULOU: I think I hear him coming.

*Enter* WILLY.

YVONNE: Hey Willy, the election victory calls you. Say something.

FLORKIN: Who's that? The landlady? Beautiful woman, by heavens!

WILLY: What is a normal man? A normal man is someone who gets up in the morning to go to work and in the evening when he comes home, he just wants to be left in peace. He eats stuff that's grown right where he lives. He'll never allow some dog to take his job away from him. And he doesn't like the smell of shit that comes from foreign countries. He knows his friends by the way they're disgusted by the same things he is, and he respects them because they're all part of the same race. He holds out his hand to them, and that hand is warm, and the other, the one that's cold, that's what he'll use to smash in the face of the first opportunist who passes by. I'm a normal man and it's normal men who voted for me. That's why I got elected! (HE *sits as though physically exhausted.*) My head's exploding. I'm heavy as a dead body. What are the symptoms of heart attack?

FREDDY: On the side where your heart is, boss. There!

WILLY: Asshole. You can be such an asshole sometimes. Go get me a pick-me-up. (FREDDY *exits, looking for something to drink.*) How's Claudia doing?

YVONNE: A lot better. Her life's been saved.

WILLY: Terrific.

YVONNE: I could have just hugged that surgeon when he said: "It's incredible, Mrs. Drissot, to see the resistance she has. Your daughter's struggling with every last drop of strength in her body! She wants to live! She's battling like a fury. Believe me, she came this close to dying!" Claudia was driving that reporter's car. A truck rammed into them from behind. I only say truck because they suppose it was a truck. But it was nighttime, and the guy got away. The police say there's not much chance of finding him. Some truck from some foreign country. What would it change anyway? The reporter's dead. Woe unto him who brings scandal in his wake. Crushed under the chassis. God punished him.

WILLY: Yvonne, Carmen wants to disappear. She wants to go off this very night with that little cretin. For good. 's worse than a bayonet through my heart!

YVONNE: She won't do it.

FREDDY: (*Coming back with the drinks.*) I had the big cheese on the phone, boss. He popped out with a good one: "Freddy, let's send all the ragheads to the ovens. We're not krauts, but all the same, we're not going to let just anybody chew off our dicks!"

YVONNE: That's disgusting!

FLORKIN: I agree with you entirely, madam.

LOULOU: (*Fearing an incident.*) Don't get all bent out of shape, Simon. It was just a joke!

FREDDY: Yeah, and anyway, he was only talking about Arabs.

FLORKIN (*To Freddy*): Young man, I have a scar on my back, the size of a bulldog's jaw. Can you imagine the man who did that to me? His Nazi uniform's carefully tucked away deep inside his closet. Today, he's some old man sitting on the grass. He just told his grandchildren not to throw their candy wrappers on the ground, that they have to keep the park clean. If that man pushed his way through that door right now, I can just see your face lighting up and you hugging him to you and saying, "How're you doing, my blood brother!?"

FREDDY: What's he getting at?

WILLY: Come on there, mister, we don't have to keep chewing over ancient history.

FLORKIN: My skin is marked up like an old Indian's. After we've been dead a hundred thousand years, I'll still remember.

WILLY: Loulou, you serve the gentleman one on the house.

YVONNE: That joke about the ragheads wasn't too bright, really!

WILLY: She's right, Freddy, you never stop with your bull-crap!

FREDDY: Bull-crap, bull-crap! The chief said it and I was just repeating it, that's all!

YVONNE: And what about hope? That kind of stuff doesn't give people any hope. We're supposed to be climbing toward the summit, not sinking down. Even when you're hitting bottom, you've got to close your eyes tight and say: I believe in happiness, I believe exclusively in the power of happiness.

WILLY: Okay, okay, here's to happiness!

FLORKIN: Who is that guy? So that's your DeWolf! Dismaying, my young friend, positively dismaying!

YVONNE: Claudia's there in her hospital bed, struggling. And meanwhile I'm here struggling with you all. (*To* FLORKIN.) We're all struggling just to get a little beauty into our lives. A little beauty. That's what we were put on earth to do. Otherwise what difference would there be between us and the animals, isn't that right sir?

FREDDY: Drink!

FLORKIN: She's alright, that woman is. She's got class!

YVONNE: (*Drinking a mouthful.*) That's good. It cuts through your body like a scalpel... (SHE *empties the glass in one swallow.*) I want you all to sit up and take note that the old lady can still pull her weight!

FREDDY: Better than a whole regiment.

YVONNE: I love going out dancing. I love parties! Claudia was dazzling. In her little white ankle socks. She was skipping out on the jetty. She was happy there on the coast. I like it when she calls for me in the middle of the night.

FREDDY: She got little tears in the corners of her eyes.

YVONNE: You get old. You lose everything you have.

FREDDY: Makes you look glamorous.

YVONNE: You certainly are a dynamic fellow.

FREDDY: I'm going to give you a hug, Yvonne. Come closer.

YVONNE: What strong arms you have!

FREDDY: Let the waltz begin!

(*Waltz.*)

YVONNE: I drank the elixir of love, and now I'm flying. I still have love under these wrinkles, Freddy, and I'd so love to give it to you!

FREDDY: You come to me and I'll just gobble up those old wrinkles. I'm the kind of guy who likes 'em all different ways.

YVONNE: Even an old broad who likes to flirt a little, right? (SHE *pulls away.*) Make way for real beauty, make way for the dream woman. It's me, a creature who can drink 'em all right up to heaven. Yvonne Drissot drinks, oh yes she does! And she doesn't care what anyone says about it. And strong? She scoffs at weakness. Me, all 120 pounds of good woman, twirling around like a ballerina at her high school prom. I dance. My belly's hard, barely any love handles. Nothing to speak of. This is a woman who feeds herself on thirteen brands of yogurt. Her body's made of granite. Just look at those legs! Yvonne Drissot's having the time of her life! Yvonne Drissot's doing pirouettes! She keeps turning, turning, turning, turning, turning turning, and all because her little Claudia's called Claudia and that little Claudia's going to come out of that coma.

LOULOU: Coffee for Yvonne.

YVONNE: Don't cry Claudia. You're going to sleep in the big bed tonight, and morning will come and papa will come too. Enter captain. "My condolences, Yvonne, there was nothing anyone could do, he died with honor." And that's the summary of my life. One day everything'll be just the way it was before. We'll be proud of ourselves. On July 21$^{st}$, we'll be out dancing in the streets, same as we do every year, yelling: "Long live the king. Long, live the queen. Long live our sovereigns."

WILLY: Freddy, put her to bed!

YVONNE: I don't want anyone putting me to bed.

FREDDY: Okay, do I put her to bed or not?

YVONNE: Everything looks weird to me today. I don't recognize anything anymore. Even the big amusement park doesn't look like fun to me.

FLORKIN: You going to be alright, miss?

YVONNE: I'm not at my best right now, I ask you kindly not to look at me.

JULIAN *enters*.

JULIAN: Carmen? Carmen?

FREDDY: What does this creep want?

JULIAN: Hey there, cellar rats. I'm here. Carmen?

FREDDY: I'll take care of him.

WILLY: Wait. On your way. Move it, buddy. It's in your own interest. Here's money. Take it. You want more? I'll double it if you want. Take, for chrissake. With that you can buy up all the whores in Brussels. And they've already got their panties off!

JULIAN: (*Calling.*) Carmen. Carmen. Carmen. Carmen.

FREDDY: He's just scum, boss, pure scum!

JULIAN: (*To* FREDDY.) Better watch out! I'm tough as an orangutan. (*HE calls once more*) Carmen!

FLORKIN: Who's that?

LOULOU: A creep. He likes making trouble.

FLORKIN: The man acts like he's been eating horsemeat. I can't wait to see what happens next.

*Enter* CARMEN.

CARMEN: You came back, Julian? I knew you'd be back. I always knew.

JULIAN: Pack your bags.

CARMEN: Who needs bags?

FREDDY: Watch out boss, better watch out. This guy's got nerve written all over him. He must not have noticed that he's crashing our little celebration.

JULIAN: I want you to pardon me. Pardon me for everything. If I slip my hand between your legs, you'll see, it'll be just as nice as before.

CARMEN: I wasn't the right one for you. My skin gives me away.

JULIAN: We've been asleep, and we didn't sleep well. Now daytime is here.

CARMEN: Let's start back at zero. Is it possible to do that? Let's try. When we're far away from this place, I can't tell you the size of the explosion we're gonna hear.

WILLY: Woman's bullshit, the lot of it. I've had enough of this. I'm Member of Parliament Willy DeWolf. You got the money to pay for her? No? Then you better choose: Get out that door, or I sic my dog on you.

JULIAN: I've still got a little child inside me. You wouldn't mind if I peed on you, Prince Charming, would you?

JULIAN *tries to pee on* WILLY*'s shoes.* FREDDY *goes over to clobber him.*

CARMEN: Tell him to stop.

FREDDY: He'll get exactly what he was looking for.

CARMEN: Freddy, stop!

FLORKIN: DeWolf, you can't just sit back and let this happen! Stop them! (*To* FREDDY.) Listen here, you lug, stop this instant! I've got a cane and I can still crack your jaw.

FREDDY: You damn kike, I'm going to straighten your kinky hair for you!

LOULOU: You leave him the hell alone!

WILLY: Alright. That's enough!

YVONNE: All that over a woman. It could turn your stomach.

FLORKIN: Well, I've seen all I care to see. I'm going.

LOULOU: I'm going with you. I've had it up to here.

THEY *exit.*

FREDDY: You're making a mistake, boss! They're vermin! They're eating our asses alive.

CARMEN: Are you okay, Julian, honey?

JULIAN: Come on. Let's get out of here. Now, I have eyes to see. I have ears to hear. We're free, and I spit on them.

WILLY: Carmen?

CARMEN: What?

WILLY: Does this mean you'll never love me?

YVONNE: If I were you, dear, I'd bow my head down and thank that man. Like this. Head lowered like a holy virgin before her lord and master. Willy, my lord, show me how to serve you better.

WILLY: You'll never love me?

CARMEN: Love you, Willy?

WILLY: Yeah, love me?

CARMEN: What does that mean, love you? What are you talking about? Love you like people really love each other?

WILLY: Love me. Yeah! Like two people who love each other.

CARMEN: Sorry, Willy, I'm going to hurt you now, and I know that's not nice. But there's not very much that's lovable about you, Willy. There's only your money you can spoil me with a little. Your money doesn't shine so bright, but at least it hasn't got any bright ideas. It doesn't care one way or the other about Jews and Arabs and Blacks! It takes things as they come. You, you sort out the whites from all the rest, and the good whites from the not-good whites. And just between us, Willy, it can't go on like that. You don't stop talking, like you actually had something to say. You're crammed so full, you're backed up inside. But there inside your skull there's nothing but old dead man's shit. And the only other thing you got is whatever life that's left in your drunken old cock, and your spinal column that you fold in eight equal parts whenever your party leader sticks his finger up your ass. So, I'm leaving you.

THEY *exit, running.*

FREDDY: This okay, boss?

WILLY: I would have given her everything, and she flings gall in my eyes!

FREDDY: You win the election, but you lose the chick.

WILLY: Shut your trap, Freddy, just shut your trap!

HE *suddenly turns over the table and stalks out.*

YVONNE: She was just a little streetwalker. She didn't even vote for him.

YVONNE *suddenly kisses* FREDDY *on the mouth and then runs off.* FREDDY *catches up to her.*

FREDDY: Come here my blue whale, come over here and get a gander at my harpoon.

YVONNE: (*Feebly.*) No, no.

*Lays her down, ravishes her, stands back up.*

FREDDY: Another win!

## SCENE EIGHT

*One year later. The street.* LOULOU *with his bag and suitcase, followed by* FLORKIN.

FLORKIN: You're leaving, you're leaving! It's just plain dumb to go away like that. I tell you frankly, it's dumb. It's the worst possible moment. Human dignity is on the rise. The people are pouring out onto the streets. They're saying no. Isn't that what you wanted? It's a year now you've been saying, "It's high time things started taking off. We've got to shake things up. We've got to shake things up." Your friend there, the waitress's daughter says, "Why should resignation be the only thing we have in common in this country?" That girl is right. I say those schemers and plotters better start trembling, 'cause they're going to get a big kick in the ass! And there'll be nothing left of all their contempt and arrogance, nothing. Finished, over, once and for all!

LOULOU: Nothing's going to happen. Look around you. Listen. It'll be just like before.

FLORKIN: Is it because of me?

LOULOU: You what?

FLORKIN: Are you leaving because of me? Just say, Simon, I'm leaving because of you. It can't be because of the year we spent together, is it? Did I drive you crazy this past year? Didn't you do whatever you wanted to? Didn't you come home whenever you felt like? Went out whenever you wanted?

LOULOU: Stop following me, you old leech.

FLORKIN: There's more than enough room for two people in the house.

LOULOU: It's your money. You earned it. Keep it for yourself.

FLORKIN: Accumulating money and dying on top of the pile doesn't interest me.

LOULOU: I like you Simon, but I can't spend my whole life living with an old trumpet player who's gotten it into his head that I'm his son.

FLORKIN: You think you look slick with that little suitcase? And your bag? Can't I even walk you to the station? Hand me that bag.

LOULOU: I want to work. I'd like to earn a living. I'd like to live somewhere where the people don't spend their whole lives hauling shit back and forth on their backs.

FLORKIN: Is it my fault you don't have any work? I don't think so kid.

LOULOU: Bye Simon. Thanks for everything.

FLORKIN: Where are you going to go?

LOULOU: I don't know.

FLORKIN: What are you going to do?

LOULOU: I don't know.

FLORKIN: You going to write?

LOULOU: Yes.

FLORKIN: You'll keep in touch?

LOULOU: Yes.

FLORKIN: You'll come back?

LOULOU: I don't know.

FLORKIN: Bye, kid.

LOULOU *goes off in the distance. Enter* CLAUDIA. SHE *has changed.* SHE *is carrying a baby against her chest.*

CLAUDIA: Mr. Florkin?

FLORKIN: Ma'am?

CLAUDIA: You don't recognize me?

FLORKIN: Ah, Claudia! How are you doing?

CLAUDIA: Living, lying, not forgetting. And you?

FLORKIN: The usual stuff that goes on inside the head of an old billy-goat. The roar of memories. Sad ones, happy ones! But, I'm back on my feet! There's no reason to lay down and die before you're dead. You've got all eternity to sleep. So, five hours a day of trumpet playing. Oh yeah. How do you like that! You've got to hear me play! Practically as good as Chet Baker himself. Well, maybe I'm exaggerating just a little, but in any case, I do my share of the work, I blow my heart out and, let's just say that imagination does the rest! Not bad, eh?

CLAUDIA: Who was that guy with the bags?

FLORKIN: That was Loulou. He's going away. He doesn't want to hang around here anymore. And he's right!

CLAUDIA: When you come right down to it, everything's even muddier than before.

FLORKIN: The Minister of the Interior said, "Everything's going to change. I'm going to see these matters through right to their conclusion." I noted it down. But they'll say anything. Do you think the pot'll ever boil over in this country?

CLAUDIA: We've got to blow on the fire.

FLORKIN: Blow? I know how to do that! I like you. You're a brave woman. I'm glad we saw each other again. Goodbye, Claudia.

*Just as* FLORKIN *is about to exit,* CLAUDIA *yells joyously.*

CLAUDIA: Mister Florkin. He's three months old! He's beautiful! He already laughs when he hears music. His name is Pietro. Pietro Gorda.

SHE *holds the child out in her arms.*

**CURTAIN**

# THE MAGNOLIA

A Play

**by**

**JACQUES DE DECKER**

## CAST

Julian, *26 years old*

Adrian, *25 years old*

Marie-Antoinette, *23 years old*

Josephine-Charlotte, *31 years old*

## SCENE ONE

*One evening, in* ADRIAN*'s apartment.*

MARIE: I'm sad, Adrian. Your one and only Marie is telling you she's sad.

ADRIAN: Why?

MARIE: Because my magnolia is shriveling. Look, it's a pitiful sight to see.

ADRIAN: It's pining away, I guess.

MARIE: What do you mean, pining away?

ADRIAN: It doesn't get to see you often enough, so it's lost its lust for life.

MARIE: Can't you manage to take better care of it for just a little longer?

ADRIAN: It's YOUR magnolia!

MARIE: That's true enough.

ADRIAN: Flowers are part of my profession. I have my hands full with my garden as it is. And now I'm supposed to supervise some potted plant to boot! You're the one who brought it over here, so you're the one who ought to be taking care of it. Besides, I've always wondered why you thought I was to be trusted with this magnolia.

MARIE: So it would have someone to look after it. But don't bother your pretty little head about it. I'll find another gardener.

ADRIAN: A better gardener than me? Impossible.

MARIE: Exactly. I thought I'd made the right choice. You saturate yourself with nature. You rise with the hens, you hit the sack with them. . .

ADRIAN: I beg to differ. Only with you Marie do I hit the sack, and if there's one thing I'm absolutely sure of, it's that you are no hen.

MARIE: You mean when I'm not here, you don't sleep at all?

ADRIAN: No, that's exactly when I concentrate on resting up.

MARIE: From what?

ADRIAN: From you!

MARIE: Thanks a lot!

ADRIAN: It's a compliment. Passion is fatiguing. It's a well known fact. I need to be at the top of my game when you get here.

MARIE: None of that explains why you can't water your magnolia.

ADRIAN: I repeat, it's not MY magnolia. It's yours. It's here on a bed and breakfast basis. Hey, that'd be a perfect name for an old cottage like this "The Magnolias." It's a name that even my mother could love.

MARIE: I demand an explanation. If you really consider this magnolia to be my property, I don't see why you'd neglect it. You don't neglect me. It's not like you. I'd have noticed. So, why then can't you do the same for this poor little magnolia?

ADRIAN: What do you want me to say?

MARIE: I think you're hiding something from me

ADRIAN: You know I never hide anything from you, Marie.

MARIE: Prove it.

ADRIAN: You'll think it's stupid.

MARIE: Cut the crap. Just spit it out.

ADRIAN: Because I don't know where it comes from.

MARIE: From the florist!

ADRIAN: You go and buy a magnolia at a florist, when you could have had any flower you ever wanted right from me?

MARIE: No, obviously.

ADRIAN: So then what? They gave it to you for free?

MARIE: Leant. Confided, if you like.

ADRIAN: Who did?

MARIE: My Gran. I thought I told you. In her hospital room, when she had that operation on her appendix, they wouldn't allow any flowers in the room, so she asked me to look after it.

ADRIAN: Why didn't you take it to your place then?

MARIE: I repeat. Because you are the country squire, the field rat, and I've always believed things should be assigned to people who have the know-how to deal with them.

ADRIAN: Well, if you put it like that. . . But then why didn't you say so to begin with?

MARIE: What?

ADRIAN: This story about your grandmother.

MARIE: You can hardly call it a story.

ADRIAN: Ok, let's back up: why am I only now hearing how this plant got here?

MARIE: Because I wanted to please you. I thought it would give you pleasure to be given a magnolia.

ADRIAN: Well, to be totally honest, it doesn't give me the least bit of pleasure!

MARIE: Then you should have told me so, and it'd have gone right back where it came from.

ADRIAN: I thought you'd take it badly.

MARIE: So now I take things badly? That takes the cake. Just the opposite, I take things perfectly well. I don't twist myself into a pretzel with all kinds of doubts and questions. You want to offer me flowers? I think it's sweet. It makes me happy. I have no problem with it.

ADRIAN: You're a woman!

MARIE: You're funny, you know that? Here's a person who talks of nothing but roses, of his thoughts, and the smell of his sweet peas, and then he claims he doesn't like flowers.

ADRIAN: I love flowers, but I don't like having someone give them to me.

MARIE: What about your onions and tulips then? I risked incurring the wrath of Dutch Customs when I brought them across the border illegally. I risked my life to get them to you.

ADRIAN: Okay, but those were onions for planting in the garden. It's not the same thing in the least!

MARIE: Is that right? And anyway, onions are the ugliest vegetable in the world. I only brought them 'cause you never stopped talking about planting onions; you seemed to have a terrible yen for them. I did wonder why on earth you wanted them so badly.

ADRIAN: Because... Because... It's none of your... magnolias!

MARIE: Very witty! Your gardening hobby has made you so creative with words. Well said!

ADRIAN: Delighted to see you so pleased. You're finally smiling.

MARIE: Yes, you've won your audience's applause with your dramaturgy. You've done it. You're a hit.

ADRIAN: Was all that a test?

MARIE: What?

ADRIAN: The bit about the magnolia. Trying to see how far you could push me?

MARIE: What exactly are you trying to prove? Adrian, let me give you a hug... What's going on with you? I've never known anyone with less self-confidence than you. Thankfully, you make up for it in the sack. That must be your rustic side.

ADRIAN: Rustic?

MARIE: Well yes, bucolic, your countrified side, I mean. Here where nature rules supreme. It's such a respite!

ADRIAN: Respite from what?

MARIE: From civilization. I love you Adrian, you know that. I love you working in your garden. I love you sitting at your table designing other peoples' gardens. I love the way you pluck me like a flower. What is it about a magnolia in a pot that would get you so uptight? I merely said it looks neglected, which is a shame. . .

ADRIAN: Why don't you take it back to your grandmother then?

MARIE: Because it's fine here, it goes perfectly with this living room. It's as though it had taken root here.

ADRIAN: I could plant it in the garden.

MARIE: No, don't. It shouldn't go one step further.

ADRIAN: You're telling me it goes well with this decor?

MARIE: For the time being, yes.

ADRIAN: Why don't you take it back with you to your place or to your office?

MARIE: My office? So the clients can use it as an ashtray? No way. I don't think so. It's fine here, same as me.

ADRIAN: But *it stays* here.

MARIE: All the more reason to take good care of it.

ADRIAN: Ok, ok, I will, don't worry. And you? Why can't you do the same?

MARIE: What?

ADRIAN: Move in here.

MARIE: And take root? You must be confusing me with a flowerpot, with some floral arrangement. I've got legs, baby!

ADRIAN: To bend up to your neck.

MARIE: That depends on the context.

ADRIAN: Seriously. You know perfectly well why I devote so much time to this garden, why I decorated the house the way I did. . .

MARIE: So that one day I'd say, "I can't tear myself away from here," is that it? But Adrian, that would take all the thrill out of my heart.

ADRIAN: What do you mean?

MARIE: When I take the exit off the highway, when I make it here in any kind of weather, as I'm driving down those little country lanes and know I'm actually going to see you in a matter of moments. . .my heart goes pit-a-pat. If I lived here, it'd dry right up. The day you finally get that through that thick skull of yours. . .

## SCENE TWO

*One night in* JULIAN*'s apartment.*

ANTOINETTE: Can't you sleep?

JULIAN: I woke up with an idea in my head, so I got it down on paper.

ANTOINETTE: That's funny. Paper.

JULIAN: I could have typed it directly on the computer, but I couldn't stand it. I hate myself when I write by computer. I think it's unfair. Almost a betrayal.

ANTOINETTE: I have a hard time seeing who you're betraying that way.

JULIAN: All those authors from the past who didn't have so much as a typewriter. Can you imagine? They wrote everything by hand. Making all those endless corrections. When they'd get to the point where it became totally illegible, they'd just recopy the whole thing. When I don't like something I write, I just press the fatal button and—wham!—it all vanishes into thin air.

ANTOINETTE: Not at all, Julian darling. Your Mac is perfectly silent. The soul of discretion, just like everything else about you. I can't even hear your mouse peep. And even better, it lights up your whole face. I open one eye and see you bathed in that blue light. Which reassures me, and I go right back to sleep.

JULIAN: Doesn't it scare you? I must look like a ghost.

ANTOINETTE: Exactly, but I love ghosts, especially at night.

JULIAN: Well then I shouldn't be studying Molière. I should be doing research on Sheridan le Fanu.

ANTOINETTE: And who is Sheridan le Fanu?

JULIAN: Someone who wrote short stories about vampires. There, fourth pile on the left, the one that's having a landslide. It's great stuff. The others may keep you awake at night, but this one would rock you to sleep.

ANTOINETTE: Am I getting in your way?

JULIAN: How could you possibly get in my way? I love it when you pop up here when I'm working at night. It's my recompense. I've got it coming.

ANTOINETTE: Coming for what?

JULIAN: For all the nights I don't see you.

ANTOINETTE: Do you miss me Julian?

JULIAN: Of course I do. I can't sleep. So I work.

ANTOINETTE: If I was around every day and every night, you'd work less.

JULIAN: That's for sure.

ANTOINETTE: So, the moral of the story's that you love me more when I'm not around!

JULIAN: I love you period. When you're here and when you're not here. Love isn't contingent on the person being present. . .and I'm not the only one who says so.

ANTOINETTE: But it's a pretty strange idea regardless.

JULIAN: Balzac had the same idea. He lived for thirty years at a huge distance from the woman he loved. Then he finally married her and proceeded to die.

ANTOINETTE: What? He died because he married her?

JULIAN: I never said that.

ANTOINETTE: You have a way of saying things without actually saying them. . .

JULIAN: You know. . .we often say one thing to mean another, or to hide others. . .

ANTOINETTE: We speak in order to lie?

JULIAN: I never said that.

ANTOINETTE: You're getting on my nerves. I'm going to sleep.

JULIAN: Stay a little longer, Antoinette.

ANTOINETTE: I'm not getting back in bed without you.

JULIAN: I'll be there in a just a second.

ANTOINETTE: You always say that, and of course, you do just the opposite; which dovetails with your theory. Which is to say that you like me better asleep.

JULIAN: I wouldn't disagree. Every so often I look at you lying there: beautiful, languid, desirable. . .

ANTOINETTE: But you never just jump on my horns. That would be too vulgar I suppose?

JULIAN: If I jumped on you every time I found you desirable, we'd be divorced before you knew it.

ANTOINETTE: We aren't even married.

JULIAN: I mean that if we were married, we'd get divorced.

ANTOINETTE: Oh really? And on what grounds?

JULIAN: Sexual harassment.

ANTOINETTE: You think so?

JULIAN: You look so funny when you say that. As if having one lover champing at the bit would never be enough, like you needed a whole regiment.

ANTOINETTE: I never said that.

JULIAN: You never said anything at all.

ANTOINETTE: So?

JULIAN: Your gestures, the scrunched up face, the tone of voice say it all. The body never lies. *Your* body never lies. You are fully present in every movement of your body; and that's why I love you.

ANTOINETTE: You just love my booty. Why don't you just say it?

JULIAN: What language!

ANTOINETTE: Might as well call a spade a spade. Besides, I might as well warn you: I only love *you* for *your* booty.

JULIAN: Thanks for the compliment.

ANTOINETTE: I thought it would offend you.

JULIAN: It didn't work. Anyway, why would it offend me?

ANTOINETTE: Because you have such a great mind. You're a scholar, a brain.

JULIAN: A brain that's interested exclusively in books about booties. Let's be precise.

ANTOINETTE: So all these books you study are just porn?

JULIAN: No, French farce. And what is it all about really, French farce?

ANTOINETTE: Infidelity, sleeping around in all its forms. I have the letters to prove it.

JULIAN: But what's at the core? What do you think it's all for, all the dramatic devices? Desire, kissing, fucking: booty!

ANTOINETTE: Yes, but only so's to make fun of it.

JULIAN: Even better! But surely there's something else too? Property. People play each other over and over because they think they belong to one another, that they owe each other things, that they're violating contracts. . . So, they make believe.

ANTOINETTE: Don't you believe that people belong to one another?

JULIAN: Good God, no. Yuck!

ANTOINETTE: Me, for example, don't I belong to you?

JULIAN: Of course not!

ANTOINETTE: Don't you wish I belonged to you?

JULIAN: Certainly not.

ANTOINETTE: That's very nice!

JULIAN: Yes, it certainly is nice.

ANTOINETTE: So, you're cheating on me?

JULIAN: How's that, cheating on you?

ANTOINETTE: I don't belong to you, so you think that you don't belong to me either, so you can do whatever you feel like, so you must be cheating on me.

JULIAN: I'm not cheating you. That would be absurd.

ANTOINETTE: Why?

JULIAN: Because if I wanted to cheat on you, that would mean I wanted to split up with you. It would be the warning bell. And I'd behave accordingly.

ANTOINETTE: In fact, you love me. It's as simple as that.

JULIAN: Exactly.

ANTOINETTE: So, why don't you ever ask me if I love you?

JULIAN: Because if I had to ask you that question, it would mean I had my doubts. Now, if I were in doubt, it'd mean I was already miserable. Because the words all by themselves would never prove that you love me.

ANTOINETTE: You might be right. You must have gone through so much to understand so much!

JULIAN: I haven't lived through anything. I've only read all the books on the subject; so the flesh is no worse for the wear. . .

ANTOINETTE: Do tell! But I thought you had something on your mind.

JULIAN: Of course I *have* something on my mind.

ANTOINETTE: Well I want to go to sleep!

JULIAN: That's not how it seemed.

## SCENE THREE

*In* JOSEPHINE-CHARLOTTE*'s pharmacy.*

JOSEPHINE-CHARLOTTE: So nice to see you. I thought you must have started going to a different pharmacy.

MARIE-ANTOINETTE: I've just been so busy, you have no idea.

JOSEPHINE-CHARLOTTE: A new research trip with your boss?

MARIE-ANTOINETTE: Are you kidding? One was enough! Never again.

JOSEPHINE-CHARLOTTE: He took you off to some exotic place, didn't he?

MARIE-ANTOINETTE: That was just the problem! If he'd taken me someplace accessible, I would have hopped the first train or plane out of there, and he'd never have seen me again for the rest of his life.

JOSEPHINE-CHARLOTTE: But still, it was nice of him to invite you.

MARIE-ANTOINETTE: If you think he did that for my personal edification! It was *his* edification he had in mind.

JOSEPHINE-CHARLOTTE: Maybe he wasn't looking forward to the trip, and was imagining you might make it easier for him, more. . . pleasant.

MARIE-ANTOINETTE: I should have told him to take you instead!

JOSEPHINE-CHARLOTTE: Me with a man? Have you taken a good look at me?

MARIE-ANTOINETTE: You could have plied him with pills, drugs, capsules, a magic potion or something. What do I know? That would have calmed him down.

JOSEPHINE-CHARLOTTE: I sincerely doubt it. The males who wind up here with those kinds of disturbances, they're pretty hardened cases. So, you never came to the poor man's rescue?

MARIE-ANTOINETTE: I'd sooner have died.

JOSEPHINE-CHARLOTTE: Really! And are you still working at the agency?

MARIE-ANTOINETTE: I told him I was getting married, and that my fiancé was very jealous, that he was a martial arts instructor, and that he'd already dangled one of my former boyfriends out the window!

JOSEPHINE-CHARLOTTE: And did he die?

MARIE-ANTOINETTE: You dope! Of course it's not true. But my boss believed it, and that's what counts. We were in darkest Japan, where the atmosphere was conducive. I told him I'd had to negotiate for fifteen days with my fiancé before obtaining permission to take off. He was flattered. And no doubt he figured out that he was lucky to be able to hold onto such a go-getter at the agency.

JOSEPHINE-CHARLOTTE: Guys really believe everything you tell them. That's why I stopped hanging out with them.

MARIE-ANTOINETTE: With you it's hormonal.

JOSEPHINE-CHARLOTTE: Perhaps, but selective. I never molested *you*, did I?

MARIE-ANTOINETTE: And a very good thing too.

JOSEPHINE-CHARLOTTE: It might be hormonal for you as well, but a bit less discriminating, if I'm not mistaken.

MARIE-ANTOINETTE: What are you talking about? I didn't let the boss screw me. Doesn't that say something?

JOSEPHINE-CHARLOTTE: Him? He doesn't count. He probably reminded you of your father.

MARIE-ANTOINETTE: Not at all! He'd have been ruled out as a father figure from the get-go. My dad's the bomb! How can you say such a thing?

JOSEPHINE-CHARLOTTE: Oh just a stab in the dark. Sorry. I've never laid eyes on either of them. Do you have a prescription?

MARIE-ANTOINETTE: No, I just came by. . . for a consultation.

JOSEPHINE-CHARLOTTE: What seems to be the trouble?

MARIE-ANTOINETTE: I'm too happy.

JOSEPHINE-CHARLOTTE: Well, everything's going swimmingly then.

MARIE-ANTOINETTE: Everything's going far too well. I have everything I want. I'm fulfilled beyond my wildest dreams.

JOSEPHINE-CHARLOTTE: So you came across the one rare bird everyone's trying so hard to find?

MARIE-ANTOINETTE: I have two birdcages.

JOSEPHINE-CHARLOTTE: Two. . . two guys? Two main squeezes at the same time? You have two lovers?

MARIE-ANTOINETTE: Is there anything wrong with that?

JOSEPHINE-CHARLOTTE: Well, if it works for you. . .

MARIE-ANTOINETTE: No! Not in the least. I just told you I've reached the mountaintop, the point beyond which there is no higher!

JOSEPHINE-CHARLOTTE: So what's the problem?

MARIE-ANTOINETTE: That it can't last. It must be ordained somewhere that one day or another, the whole thing'll go up in smoke.

JOSEPHINE-CHARLOTTE: Have you taken precautions?

MARIE-ANTOINETTE: I take the pill, and they wear condoms.

JOSEPHINE-CHARLOTTE: Yuck!

MARIE-ANTOINETTE: You carry some very cute ones now, and tasty into the bargain.

JOSEPHINE-CHARLOTTE: That's not what I was talking about. How do you arrange it all?

MARIE-ANTOINETTE: It's not really complicated. As far as they know, I'm sleeping over at my parents', which isn't altogether untrue: I still have a room there. I told them I couldn't give them the number since it was hush-hush. That dad works for the Secret Service.

JOSEPHINE-CHARLOTTE: And they swallowed that?

MARIE-ANTOINETTE: Why not? They can call me at my office. And there, it's not a problem; they can find me whenever they need to. And if I'm not in, they can leave a message or someone tells them when I'll be back. Whether they ask for Marie or Antoinette.

JOSEPHINE-CHARLOTTE: How's that?

MARIE-ANTOINETTE: To the one I'm Marie and to the other Antoinette. My colleagues are used to clients only remembering your first name.
May I please speak to Marie?
Oh, Marie-Antoinette!
Can I speak to Antoinette please?
Oh, Marie-Antoinette!
And I just tell them it's an in-joke—me having a famous name of the most famous queen in history.

JOSEPHINE-CHARLOTTE: Is that really called for. . . ?

MARIE-ANTOINETTE: It's crucial. This way I'm not technically pulling the wool over anybody's eyes. In the one case I'm Marie; in the other, Antoinette. It's just delightful. You should give it a try. I can imagine the life you'd have if you were Josephine to some, Charlotte to others, and Josephine-Charlotte all the way around.

JOSEPHINE-CHARLOTTE: I'd need to give it some thought. . . women are too damn sneaky. While men: lambs to slaughter!

MARIE-ANTOINETTE: The nicest lambs, if you ask me!

JOSEPHINE-CHARLOTTE: Sounds like you've broken the mold. It's been so long since I've done anything like that. But, tell me—don't they suspect anything? Don't they miss having you all to themselves?

MARIE-ANTOINETTE: One does. He wants to settle down. The other is pretty much resigned to the way things are.

JOSEPHINE-CHARLOTTE: So the first one is more clingy than the other, would you say?

MARIE-ANTOINETTE: The resigned one?

JOSEPHINE-CHARLOTTE: Sure sounds that way, yes.

MARIE-ANTOINETTE: And do you like 'em resigned?

JOSEPHINE-CHARLOTTE: Not really.

MARIE-ANTOINETTE: You see!

JOSEPHINE-CHARLOTTE: So why don't you ditch him?

MARIE-ANTOINETTE: He's so cute. And so cuddly. A total teddy bear, you have no idea. When I'm at his place, it's like being on a farm.

JOSEPHINE-CHARLOTTE: Or in a stable. . . speaking of lambs!

MARIE-ANTOINETTE: Very witty I'm sure! No, that's not it. He lives in the country. He designs gardens, grows flowers. . . In the winter, we go into hibernation under gigantic quilts; and when the good weather returns, we sleep with the window open and wake to the sound of the first rooster crowing.

JOSEPHINE-CHARLOTTE: You must wind up in horrendous traffic jams trying to get back into town.

MARIE-ANTOINETTE: I'm the first one in the office, to make up for the other days, when I get there at ten thirty, tail between my legs.

JOSEPHINE-CHARLOTTE: So, you've got two whole different biorhythms!

MARIE-ANTOINETTE: What do you call it?

JOSEPHINE-CHARLOTTE: Biorhythms! It's as if your body functions two different ways. If that works for you, then bully.

MARIE-ANTOINETTE: Yes, but I'm petrified. . . that it might all go kerflooey. The whole arrangement's wound so tight.

JOSEPHINE-CHARLOTTE: How long has this been going on now?

MARIE-ANTOINETTE: I got to know Adrian first. He came to my aid when I broke down. I'd driven into a ditch only a couple of yards from his house. It was February. Shortly after I dumped Damian.

JOSEPHINE-CHARLOTTE: I really liked him. Did you know that he stops by to see me from time to time? He's so polite. Misses you a lot. I usually have to throw him out—but ever so gently.

MARIE-ANTOINETTE: I would have hung onto him, but I was still buried under such a high code of ethics at the time. And then I ran into Julian in the library. In early March, to be precise.

JOSEPHINE-CHARLOTTE: So it's been going on two months. There's no good reason to stop now. . . Two months for a relationship of this kind is practically an eternity!

## SCENE FOUR

*One evening in* JULIAN*'s apartment.*

JULIAN: I sometimes tell myself it's crazy living in town, doing the job I do. It's not a 9 to 5 kind of thing; I get three quarters of my work done at home, or at the library, that is, when it's not being renovated or if they're having a strike. Thanks to my Mac, I can log on wherever I am. For people like me it's no problem to live in the country.

ANTOINETTE: Aren't you the one who once said that it was absurd to move towns to the countryside?

JULIAN: Not me, I was quoting someone else. A friend of Feydeau's. A certain Allais. I was saying something like "Cities would be a whole lot less crowded if only they moved them to the country." He was just being funny, of course. But today, everything's transformed. Thanks to computers, you can connect to whomever you want, wherever you want. You're the only one who never tires of being obsolete.

ANTOINETTE: Obso-late?

JULIAN: Obsolete. Ob-so-lete. Antoinette. Left in the dust, outdated.

ANTOINETTE: Outdated, me?

JULIAN: 'Cause you hate talking on the phone, you haven't even opened an account. And when I call you at the office you blow me off. Three seconds of your precious time if I'm lucky—that's my daily quota.

ANTOINETTE: The telephone is my daily bread.

JULIAN: You sound like a phone sex professional.

ANTOINETTE: If I've got you on my line, then there's no room for my clients. But I'm going to enter the modern world and buy a cell-phone. Then I'll be universally connected, and you can reach me wherever you want.

JULIAN: Wherever *you* want, you mean. I'll call you, but I'll never know where you actually are. I really can't believe my ears. You go around everywhere complaining how telephones are totally yucko . . . and now you expect me to believe you'd be happy to be intruded on anywhere and everywhere?

ANTOINETTE: This is a totally different matter. I won't be glued to the phone. It's the phone that'll follow me around. For a nomad like me, it's the perfect solution, don't you think? I suddenly realized that the guy who invented cell phones made them exactly with me in mind.

JULIAN: Well, we'll see. If I could find a place in the country, better still with a little garden, I think I'd be a whole lot happier.

ANTOINETTE: And what am I supposed to do? Spend my whole life stuck in traffic jams on the highway? Thanks, but no thanks!

JULIAN: As if you'd be coming every day. . . We might see each other somewhat less often, but it'd be more quality time. I'm sure our relationship would be the stronger for it.

ANTOINETTE: Frankly, I can't see you living outside some hick town, cut off from libraries and theatres. You're a city rat, Julian, I told you that before. I bet if you were to move, you'd be bored stiff in no time, and you'd be hightailing it back here in no time flat. I know you that well.

JULIAN: You'd be surprised.

ANTOINETTE: And besides, I don't know if I'd really like you in that case. I can't picture you pruning roses and watering the magnolias. . .

JULIAN: Got it. And while we're on the subject, how is your magnolia anyway? I hope you're keeping it well-tended.

ANTOINETTE: It's in excellent hands. My grandmother dotes on it.

JULIAN: You gave it to your grandmother?

ANTOINETTE: Leant it. Sent it to boarding school. Flowers thrive with her. She exudes long life.

JULIAN: How old is she?

ANTOINETTE: Eighty-five. Stands straight as a rod. In excellent condition. Never had an operation in her life. A force of nature. Everything she touches—animals, plants, flowers—all prosper and flourish.

JULIAN: I'd like to get to know her. I like old people. I find them much more interesting than. . .

ANTOINETTE: Than me, is that what you mean?

JULIAN: Don't make fun of me. If your grandmother is anything like you, she must be quite something. And your grandfather?

ANTOINETTE: That's a real mystery. In fact, I've got two. And they both claim to be my mother's father.

JULIAN: One close look would surely resolve the question.

ANTOINETTE: Actually no. The top half of her face is like the one and the bottom half the other. She's short sighted like one and left handed like the other. A true family enigma! But my mother's made out like a bandit. She was spoiled rotten by the two of them, whose only aim in life was to lavish her with whatever she wanted.

JULIAN: Weird story. . . When you come across these seemingly ordinary old people, you have no idea how bizarre they can actually be. Anyway, I'm convinced that when they were our age, they were much more whack than we are. You only have to read Feydeau. They really knew how to yuck it up! But these days we're as serious as the pope. Everything is too regimented and heavily administered. Even vacation time. . . yes, especially vacations. You should know something about it, you who sell group tours.

ANTOINETTE: Which is why I never suggested you go on one. That said, you could stand some shaking up. You can't keep your head buried in paperwork forever. . .

JULIAN: Don't worry. The season is beginning again.

ANTOINETTE: What season?

JULIAN: The water polo season.

ANTOINETTE: You play water polo?

JULIAN: As soon as it warms up a bit. Out in the open.

ANTOINETTE: Oh really. I somehow never saw you doing that.

JULIAN: You learn something new every day, princess.

ANTOINETTE: You, with a little cap on, in the waves, chasing after a ball? I'm totally floored. And where is it you do this?

JULIAN: In a club just outside town. I'd take you along, but it's men only.

ANTOINETTE: Men-only clubs still exist? Like in the time of dinosaurs?

JULIAN: Have you ever seen a co-ed game of football? Well, this is just the same, only with water!

ANTOINETTE: You're kidding! I'd never have imagined!

JULIAN: It's a day for revelations, I see.

ANTOINETTE: And that's what's giving you this urge to emigrate?

JULIAN: That and one other thing. I want to apply myself to some major research project. Something serious, really heavy. I don't think I can do that in town. There are just too many distractions here. It's all too frenzied.

ANTOINETTE: Frenzied, you? I've never seen anyone so stable.

JULIAN: It's hard to hold onto it. And I spend my whole time dreaming of foliage. You never see so much as a tree around here. Of course there is that terrace. . .

ANTOINETTE: The terrace?

JULIAN: That you see from the window, right over there.

ANTOINETTE: You talking about the roof of that little garage down there?

JULIAN: Or if I don't move away, I could imagine planting a kind of hanging garden out there.

ANTOINETTE: A hanging garden? Are you crazy or what? You'd have to haul several tons of dirt up there for starters. If you want to murder your neighbor then be my guest! And that's not even taking into consideration how much it would cost. How would you get the water to drain? How would you seal the damn thing? You'd need to hire an engineer, get a building permit, official permission from the city government.

JULIAN: Oh for God's sake! It slipped my mind that I had a resident expert here!

ANTOINETTE: Would you like a little piece of advice? Just forget it. If you really must have greenery in your life, I'll bring the magnolia back: that way you'll have your own little miniature garden. . .

## SCENE FIVE

*One evening in* ADRIAN*'s house. . .*

MARIE: Say, Adrian?

ADRIAN: Yeah. . . ?

MARIE: Do I bore you?

ADRIAN: Why would you think you bore me, my darling? It's just that if you'd given me a heads-up, I'd've told you not to come tonight. I have this plan I've got to get done ASAP, and it must look like I'm neglecting you. I'm delighted you're here, beside me, while I work. . . but you must excuse me if I don't raise my head. You know how these companies are. You don't hear a peep out of them for two years and then all of a sudden they snap to and it's urgent, needed immediately, because the board of some agency's got to have it in five minutes. Long story short, I'm stressed.

MARIE: What is this plan?

ADRIAN: A public park, in the city. It's a big break for my career.

MARIE: So now you're talking in terms of career?

ADRIAN: A chance like this doesn't turn up twice. And I'm loaded with ideas for it.

MARIE: Is it in the center of town?

ADRIAN: No, just outside. And I know the neighborhood real well. Right next to the swimming pool?

MARIE: What swimming pool?

ADRIAN: The one where I go to play water polo when the weather improves. Open air of course. I can't stand indoor pools. And the only club where they play open air water polo is right there, close by. I've passed by the property a million times. Used to be private, but this city agency bought it up. So they're constructing a park there. I'm sure I'll get the commission; I know the site like the back of my hand. I don't care for this kind of competition, but in this case, I almost get the feeling that it's all laid out with my name on it. Do you see what I mean, Marie? Honest, if you'd called me, I would have told you the whole thing. The last thing I'd want to do is neglect a visitor, but. . .

MARIE: A visitor? What do you mean by that? So now I'm just a visitor!?

ADRIAN: Naturally, so long as you don't live here, I'm bound to see it from that angle. It's always like a party when you show up. I prepare for hours in advance. . . But this time, nothing. I haven't even done any shopping. We'll have to make do with whatever leftovers we can scrounge in the fridge. I swear to you, my head is spinning.

MARIE: No problem, Adrian. It happens. . . Tell me, that water polo club of yours, is it co-ed?

ADRIAN: Co-ed? Don't make me laugh! You know what a football game is like? Well, it's the same thing, except that it's played in water.

MARIE: So? Don't women know how to swim? Don't they know how to play with a ball?

ADRIAN: Shall I draw you a sketch?

MARIE: No, no extra sketches needed. Anyway, you'd use up all your pencils. I get the idea, I get it!

ADRIAN: You're not going to sulk just because the club doesn't accept women, are you?

MARIE: Oh, that's just the way it is. It's been going on for thousands of years anyway. . .

ADRIAN: Water polo was invented in eighteen hundred and. . . I don't know the exact date.

MARIE: No worries. I'm just pulling your leg, Adrian. You live out here in the open air, you're bursting with good health, you're getting away from all the stress. . . and you drive into town to keep up your fitness routine. It's all a little topsy-turvy, isn't it?

ADRIAN: Does my doing water polo bother you?

MARIE: No, it's a hoot. I can just see you wearing your little cap, throwing your little ball at your little friends. You're such adolescents.

ADRIAN: Who, us?

MARIE: Men, or rather those who claim to be.

ADRIAN: What did you eat today?

MARIE: A salad. And that, at least, was co-ed. . . I mean mixed.

ADRIAN: Marie, I beg you, I have to hand in this project first thing tomorrow morning. I have no choice. It's just the way it is.

MARIE: So work. Don't pay any attention to me. Just act as if I wasn't even here.

*Silence.*

ADRIAN: It's not exactly easy to act like you're not here, believe me.

MARIE: Do you want me to go?

ADRIAN: No, absolutely not! Let it never be said that I'd let you take off on an evening when you came to see me. I could never forgive myself.

MARIE: Basically, what is needed here is a stand-in. When you're too busy, I'd have some company and you'd get some peace. . . Did you hear what I just said?

ADRIAN: No, I hit a bad glitch there. I wasn't really listening. I'm sorry.

MARIE: I was saying: there needs to be another man in my life, to replace you when you're not available. That way everyone'll be happy. A sort of body double. . . You must have that in water polo, like a pinch hitter.

ADRIAN: No, Marie. I'd never put up with anything like that.

MARIE: Because I'm your property? Is that how you see it?

ADRIAN: Not at all. That has nothing to do with it. It's just that when you're close as we are, it's hard to share. If you share, then you lose the sense of the whole.

MARIE: Explain.

ADRIAN: If I had the time I would. I'd really like to clarify my thinking on the subject. But frankly, it's all pretty complicated. I just don't feel it's right. I simply don't feel it, alright? And that's that.

MARIE: Adrian, my darling, I have a feeling I just made the sky fall down on your head.

ADRIAN: Not at all, no, I've never been able to multi-task. So, to design my park and hold forth on a double life, I'm afraid, is quite beyond me.

MARIE: All I can tell is that you're against it.

ADRIAN: Against what?

MARIE: The idea of having a stand-in.

ADRIAN: I just have to think about it, as far as I *can* think about it at all, and it's like I get a lump. Come and feel, right there. No, that's not right. I'm sorry.

MARIE: How could you possibly have a double in any case, Adrian darling? You're unique. That's why I love you. Listen, what I'm going to do is go and say hi to my grandmother. In any case, you're not going to get unstuck from this table all night, that's obvious.

ADRIAN: How's your grandmother doing anyway? Has she got back from the hospital?

MARIE: It was only a little fibroid tumor.

ADRIAN: A fibroid? You said it was her appendix. That did surprise me at her age.

MARIE: Yes of course, what was I thinking? Her appendix. I've got a little surprise for her, and she'll be so happy about it.

ADRIAN: You mean having you turn up like that, right out of the blue?

MARIE: No, to bring her back her magnolia!

## SCENE SIX

*Beside the swimming pool.*

JULIAN: You took a break too? You don't realize ahead of time, but once you stop doing it, it's so hard to get back to the same level, isn't it?

ADRIAN: I didn't get to swim enough over the winter. Ruins your stamina.

JULIAN: Me neither. I saw right from the start I'd never make it to halftime.

ADRIAN: I hate indoor pools; I feel like a goldfish; they make me suffocate!

JULIAN: You and me both. I can't stand swimming pools in general. I dream of swimming in ponds and rivers, like back in the day. . .

ADRIAN: What day?

JULIAN: At the turn of the last century, before 1914. Swimming pools barely existed then.

ADRIAN: You remember how it was back then?

JULIAN: It's not that I remember it, but I've studied the period. I've been delving into it seriously for quite some time.

ADRIAN: Are you an historian?

JULIAN: In a way. You?

ADRIAN: Garden architect.

JULIAN: Nice line of work. I've always loved the term. It's so contradictory.

ADRIAN: Oh yes?

JULIAN: Well, yes. You'd think a garden was something that grows all on its own, making all its own decisions. But when you figure there's an architect behind it all. . .

ADRIAN: There are no gardens without architects. The English have it down to a science. They make it look as if a tree popped up by chance right in the middle of a lawn, but in fact the whole thing has been planned down to the last inch.

JULIAN: Just like with plays! That's what I've studied more than anything else; good plays are put together just like a musical score, but the audience has no idea.

ADRIAN: Exactly. You can't see how it's done if it's done well.

JULIAN: This is weird isn't it? Here we are sitting next to a swimming pool. We don't know each other, we're suddenly on a friendly basis. . . and come to find out we think exactly alike about everything. . . I'm Julian.

ADRIAN: About everything . . . that might be going too far. I'm Adrian. Were you here last season?

JULIAN: I took a break. I had a thesis to finish. You kind of have to when you're on scholarship. It's to be expected that I'd be out of breath when you come to think of it. You should never take a break from an exercise routine. . .

ADRIAN: They seem to be managing just fine without us.

JULIAN: What a lesson in humility!

ADRIAN: We'd better get some training in to get back to par.

JULIAN: So before, you didn't play?

ADRIAN: This, oh no. I used to swim and play rugby. Until one day I realized there was a way to combine the two. So what brought you to water polo?

JULIAN: I'd had it with swimming. You're so all alone with yourself. I already spend too much time alone as it is. . .

ADRIAN: Single?

JULIAN: In a way.

ADRIAN: Me too. Well, I have someone I see from time to time, but. . .

JULIAN: So do I.

ADRIAN: Really!

JULIAN: I was referring mostly to my job: always drowning in books, you feel like you're turning into a hermit. Then, the solitary swimming thing, it's like pacing the floor of a cloister cell. I thought that a team sport would work better for me. At least in your job you meet people.

ADRIAN: Not too sure about that. Clients have to be sold on ideas, colleagues at work. . . they're not what you'd call real company. At least here, we're all in the same pool together. There's no power game.

JULIAN: Who knows! Will you just look at them, how worked up they are!

ADRIAN: I think I'm getting my second wind. I'm going to go get back in the game.

JULIAN: There's something I need to talk to you about. The gardens you do, is it always large-sized ones?

ADRIAN: Oh, well, not so big as all that. From five hundred to a thousand square yards gives you something to work with. I have a project for the park next door. It's only about an acre. You have no idea what I can do with that. I bet the people walking in it will feel like they've gotten lost in the woods.

JULIAN: And seven square yards, could you do something with that?

ADRIAN: Seven hundred square yards? Well it's doable I suppose.

JULIAN: No, no. I said seven, not seven hundred: five plus two, two times three plus one.

ADRIAN: Seven square yards? What, a bonsai garden, you mean?

JULIAN: If you like.

ADRIAN: It could be interesting. A challenge, in a way. I wouldn't mind trying it. Is it a flat piece of ground?

JULIAN: Absolutely flat. A terrace.

ADRIAN: Ah, that complicates matters. You'd have to haul up tons of earth, shore it all up, work things out with your neighbors. . . Still, it could be fun. I'll give it some thought. Is it far from here?

JULIAN: Right in the center of town.

ADRIAN: Now I understand. If you love nature, it must be horrible being holed up in a couple of square yards. I've even seen vertical gardens. . .

JULIAN: Mine will be a hanging garden.

ADRIAN: Fine. Tomorrow morning I have to see someone at the main office so I could stop by your place, if that works for you.

JULIAN: Perfect. Eleven o'clock, eleven thirty? We can have a drink.

ADRIAN: Alcohol free!

JULIAN: At that time of the morning, yes we'd better.

ADRIAN: Fine. Well, I can't make any promises. What you're asking me to do is to construct a pyramid on its point. But it's worth a shot. . . Shall we get back in?

JULIAN: They seem to be quite happy without us.

ADRIAN: I think we're going to be like two dogs in a game of skittles.

JULIAN: True that. Well, at least we've had a chance to get to know each other.

ADRIAN: You have a lot of friends?

JULIAN: Not really. My girlfriend takes up most of the space.

ADRIAN: You just said you hardly ever see her.

JULIAN: Even so, she's high maintenance.

ADRIAN: Mine too, tell you the truth. We're not married, but she's always on my mind.

JULIAN: That's why, no doubt.

ADRIAN: What?

JULIAN: If you were married, you wouldn't give her a second thought.

ADRIAN: Not in her case. I don't think it would change much. She'd always be just as much of a burden. But don't get me wrong, I'm not complaining. . .

JULIAN: You took the words right out of my mouth. There are women like that, who fill the whole landscape. Even taken in homeopathic doses.

ADRIAN: Exactly. Even if I saw more of her I still wouldn't get used to her.

JULIAN: What's she called then?

ADRIAN: Marie

JULIAN: That's nice and basic. It's ecological.

ADRIAN: And yours?

JULIAN: Antoinette.

ADRIAN: That's another thing entirely. . . obviously.

## SCENE SEVEN

*Late afternoon, in* ADRIAN*'s house.*

MARIE: Boy, it feels good to be here.

ADRIAN: Is it for the over-all tan that you say that?

MARIE: God, no. I don't need to embarrass myself. And anyway, uniformity isn't my thing! I like keeping my ass-cheeks white.

ADRIAN: No argument there. White ass-cheeks are cute, especially yours.

MARIE: Whose are you comparing them with then?

ADRIAN: Oh, I don't get all that many opportunities. But I love the "little girl" side of it. Reminds me of that ad for tanning cream. A little girl's running and a little dog's pulling down her panties, like this, with his teeth. And you can see her pale white buttocks sticking out.

MARIE: Ads for dirty old men! I take it you see yourself as the puppy. Confess—what you really want is to tear my panties off with your teeth.

ADRIAN: With my teeth? Hey, I'd never thought of that.

MARIE: You don't think about it, but it's lurking inside your head all the same. How do you think publicity works? Everything we do at the agency is based on that idea. We publish family photos, everything tasteful and wholesome, never a hint of anything indecent. Couples holding hands, going off into the sunset. But people couldn't care less. That's not what they see at all.

ADRIAN: Oh really? So what do they see?

MARIE: Guys and broads whooping it up and sending each other shooting into the air like wild animals.

ADRIAN: They must be delusional.

MARIE: It's not what you'd see, Adrian. You're a simple soul. You don't have a shred of perversity in your body. But you're atypical, the exception that proves the rule. You stand outside the general run of humanity.

ADRIAN: What do you mean, outside humanity?

MARIE: A sociological outlier, I mean. That's why I like you so much.

ADRIAN: If I follow you, couples who go on a trip together are fantasizing they'll stumble on somebody else entirely once they get to the beach.

MARIE: First of all, what exactly is a beach? The sea foam is just one vast bed stretching to infinity. And the coconut palms, haven't you ever wondered what they really are?

ADRIAN: Phallic symbols no doubt?

MARIE: One up for Adrian. So you're not as dumb as I thought, kiddo!

ADRIAN: Delighted to hear it. So if I understand correctly, I'm the noble savage.

MARIE: When you think about it, yes, something like that.

ADRIAN: So that makes you my very own concubine who comes over because she likes slumming it.

MARIE: Where did you ever get that?

ADRIAN: A friend from water polo. A client too, but he started out as a friend. He studies the turn of the century.

MARIE: The what? The turn of the century?

ADRIAN: At each turn of the century, as now, many things are in flux. . .but for him it's the end of the last century that is of prime interest.

MARIE: An historian then.

ADRIAN: Yes, but a special one. He reads plays, nothing but plays, and through them he tries to understand how people used to live.

MARIE: Fascinating! And you say he's a good client as well. . .

ADRIAN: Yes, he wants me to do a garden for him. Part of one. No earth, nothing that actually grows, and it has to be tiny to boot.

MARIE: What a weird idea. Did you go and see him?

ADRIAN: Yes, this morning. His place is packed with books. Being in the city depresses him he said. But he can't leave it.

MARIE: Why?

ADRIAN: The woman he's with doesn't want to.

MARIE: He's married?

ADRIAN: No, but his girlfriend takes up a good part of his life. I noticed that he says "girlfriend" and not "partner." Just like me in fact.

MARIE: Do you also think I take up a large part of your life?

ADRIAN: No, but. . .

MARIE: Oh, so I don't take up any room then?

ADRIAN: Stop talking nonsense, will you? I only said that when I mention you, I also tend to say "girlfriend" and not "partner." By the way, he thought your name was really cool.

MARIE: You must have really bonded to be telling him about me. What else did he say about my name?

ADRIAN: He thought it was "ecological." Seeing his apartment —if you can call it an apartment—I could understand better why you like joining me out here. A place like that, I swear you could never stand it. And as for the tanning, it's safe to say that if I do make this garden for him, his girlfriend'll feel like she's on display in a shop window.

MARIE: I wouldn't mind that.

ADRIAN: I don't think so. And from what I saw, that's not the kind of girlfriend he has either.

MARIE: But you saw the photo.

ADRIAN: That's another way, I have to say, that she resembles you—the way she clearly hated being photographed. But I can't imagine where he'd put any photos, since his books take every inch of space. I saw just one flower, a single solitary bloom. You couldn't miss it.

MARIE: Why?

ADRIAN: It was a magnolia. It's crazy how one magnolia can look just like another. It was the spitting image of the one you took to your grandmother.

MARIE: Didn't you ask him where it came from?

ADRIAN: No, should I have?

MARIE: Certainly not. It's not the kind of thing you ask. It's indiscreet. Show some respect for a person's private life for crying out loud! Of course, you compared girlfriends, that's to be expected. But comparing magnolias? Shocking!

ADRIAN: I'll ask him the next time if you want me to.

MARIE: Your next polo match?

ADRIAN: No, when he comes here, to see my plans. He was really curious to see where I lived.

MARIE: When's he coming?

ADRIAN: Do you want to meet him? I'd really like you to get to know him. He's coming the day after tomorrow to pick me up before the match and then bring me back afterwards.

MARIE: The day after tomorrow? Impossible. I have a seminar.

ADRIAN: That's strange.

MARIE: What's strange? Me saying that?

ADRIAN: Nothing, it's just that it's never happened before.

MARIE: What?

ADRIAN: You giving me a reason for your absence.

MARIE: Then this is a red-letter day. We should make a wish!

ADRIAN: What I wish for is. . .

MARIE: Don't say it out loud. It'd be bad luck!

## SCENE EIGHT

*One evening in* JULIAN*'s apartment*

ANTOINETTE: You know sometimes I think you're different from all the others.

JULIAN: I should certainly hope so!

ANTOINETTE: The other "intellectuals" I mean.

JULIAN: I'm not an intellectual.

ANTOINETTE: Aren't you though? You spend your life surrounded by books, you wear glasses like magnifying glasses. . .

JULIAN: I could wear contact lenses, if you'd rather.

ANTOINETTE: Not on your life! I like taking them off too much, you know that. I adore that short-sighted look you give me. Makes me melt.

JULIAN: You never said that before. Where did it come from?

ANTOINETTE: Sometimes you just have to be in the right mood.

JULIAN: Are you feeling guilty about something?

ANTOINETTE: No. Why?

JULIAN: I don't know. First you went into raptures about my ever-expanding bald spot, and now it's my squinty eyes. Next it'll be my knock-knees and flat feet?

ANTOINETTE: You forgot your sunken chest and your potbelly.

JULIAN: But seriously, are you fishing for compliments or what?

ANTOINETTE: Could be. I want you to tell me things.

JULIAN: What kind of things? To go on about your royal bearing, that goddess-like body of yours, your golden locks. . .

ANTOINETTE: I'd like you to talk about my soul.

JULIAN: Your soul? In the first, I don't know what that means. . .

ANTOINETTE: And in the second place, you're not so sure I even have one.

JULIAN: It's true that centuries ago there was never any question. But in this day and age, we enjoy the privilege of wondering if things of that nature exist.

ANTOINETTE: That's a given. But I'm not joking. Really. I want you to tell me how you perceive me.

JULIAN: I met a guy. . .

ANTOINETTE: You're changing the subject.

JULIAN: Not in the least. I'm right on target. You'll see. So, I met this guy—really nice—at water polo. I'll introduce you. Anyway, you're sure to meet him since he's going to be slaving away here.

ANTOINETTE: Here? What's he going to be doing here?

JULIAN: Making a garden.

ANTOINETTE: You found a nutcase who agreed to do that?

JULIAN: He's not a nutcase. He's a totally serious guy who clearly knows what he's doing to the nth degree. He designs gardens; that's such an amazing skill-set. He does a whole bunch of interesting stuff. Right now he's working on a park not far from the swimming pool.

ANTOINETTE: I don't see the connection.

JULIAN: Well, I talked with the guy alongside the pool. He told me about his wife—well his fiancée. He's not actually married. . . his girlfriend I guess. He said something actually rather beautiful. He said he could never get used to her.

ANTOINETTE: He said that?

JULIAN: Word for word. That's what struck me; I promised myself I'd remember it.

ANTOINETTE: That doesn't necessarily mean they don't get along.

JULIAN: Not at all! Quite the opposite, I'm sure. . . or at least that's how it came across to me. It meant that she'd always surprise him, that their relationship would never become banal or ordinary. That together they'd go from one surprise to the next. It struck me because I have exactly the same feeling with you. I never get used to you either, and I think it's great.

ANTOINETTE: You never said such a thing before Julian. I'm really touched.

JULIAN: Truth is, I'm plagiarizing. He was the one who said it, not me. . .

ANTOINETTE: Makes no difference. I'm really moved, all the same.

JULIAN: You aren't going to cry over it, are you?

ANTOINETTE: I just find it really moving. The two of you there, poolside in swimming trunks, with your little bathing caps on. And you suddenly start talking about the women you love, and go deep, real deep. It's as though I could see you there, right in front of my eyes, so clearly. He saying he'll never get used to her. You thinking the same thing.

JULIAN: It's like a picture out of a comic strip. He speaks, I think. For him a bubble, for me a little cloud. But I never thought it'd have such an effect on you.

ANTOINETTE: It's nothing. It'll pass. . . Oh, you men!

JULIAN: I really don't see what's so earth-shattering about it.

ANTOINETTE: You just don't get it.

JULIAN: You still haven't said why I'm not like the others.

ANTOINETTE: The other intellectuals, I said. You want proof? You play water polo and you socialize with a gardener.

JULIAN: A gardener can't be an intellectual? He lets the gardens take shape in his head first. This guy's more like a poet.

ANTOINETTE: What's his name?

JULIAN: Adrian; and his girlfriend, Marie. It's funny, isn't it?

ANTOINETTE: I don't see the humor in it.

JULIAN: He deals with plants, and she has the most beautiful first name in the world.

ANTOINETTE: You think?

JULIAN: You're not going to start sniveling again just because I said that, are you? Marie might not be the most original name you could choose, but it's definitely primal. Ecological.

ANTOINETTE: So you don't like Antoinette?

JULIAN: Yes, I love it, but it's less—how shall I put it? Less basic. That said, the two go very well together. Marie-Antoinette. Not bad, hunh? But Antoinette-Marie is hard to imagine. That's what I meant to say.

ANTOINETTE: You mean that you can't switch them round?

JULIAN: If you say so. . . But it looks like it's getting you down. Are you sad Antoinette?

ANTOINETTE: No, Antoinette isn't sad.

## SCENE NINE

*In* JOSEPHINE-CHARLOTTE*'s pharmacy.*

MARIE-ANTOINETTE: Red alert! Red alert!

JOSEPHINE-CHARLOTTE: What's going on now?

MARIE-ANTOINETTE: Adrian and Julian! They saw each other.

JOSEPHINE-CHARLOTTE: You ran into one in the street when you were arm in arm with the other?

MARIE-ANTOINETTE: You should know that I'd never walk in the street with a man. And I never let them take my arm. It gives the wrong impression.

JOSEPHINE-CHARLOTTE: What then?

MARIE-ANTOINETTE: I'm telling you they saw each other!

JOSEPHINE-CHARLOTTE: They saw each other? Ok, fine. Who told you they knew who the other was?

MARIE-ANTOINETTE: They saw each other and there's more.

JOSEPHINE-CHARLOTTE: What, they slept together!

MARIE-ANTOINETTE: Fool! No, what a horrible thought!

JOSEPHINE-CHARLOTTE: Nothing horrible about it, a man with a man, a woman with a woman. It's perfectly normal.

MARIE-ANTOINETTE: I mean that they saw each other, and they're going to see each other again!

JOSEPHINE-CHARLOTTE: So? So long as you're not there. . .

MARIE-ANTOINETTE: Yes, but they're talking about us, about me. . .

JOSEPHINE-CHARLOTTE: What do you think men talk about? Football, cars and broads! If they're discussing your butt, take it as flattery.

MARIE-ANTOINETTE: It's worse than that. They're talking about my soul.

JOSEPHINE-CHARLOTTE: Now, that, considering where things stand, is pretty catastrophic. Poor little Marie, poor little Antoinette. . . Which one is taking it worse?

MARIE-ANTOINETTE: Both of them. It's going to turn out badly.

JOSEPHINE-CHARLOTTE: There's one simple solution. You ditch one of them, so the other's none the wiser. Marie's done, Antoinette's over. You choose. You pick the best one and show your hand. The one cries, the other laughs. Life is a struggle. May the best man win!

MARIE-ANTOINETTE: What a load of crap. In the first place, I have no desire to choose. And even supposing I did, I'd go on seeing the two of them together, no matter which one I'd chosen, and that would be a catastrophe.

JOSEPHINE-CHARLOTTE: Ok, well then ditch them both.

MARIE-ANTOINETTE: You're out of your mind! I just told you I want them both.

JOSEPHINE-CHARLOTTE: Well, when a person's too greedy. . .

MARIE-ANTOINETTE: Easy to say when you're monogamous.

JOSEPHINE-CHARLOTTE: One thing at a time: not a bad principle for managing your life and family situation.

MARIE-ANTOINETTE: Family?

JOSEPHINE-CHARLOTTE: If you'd let me get a word in edgewise, you'd know that we have some big plans, Lorraine and me. We want children.

MARIE-ANTOINETTE: What? And how are you going to go about getting them?

JOSEPHINE-CHARLOTTE: Same way everyone else does I guess.

MARIE-ANTOINETTE: And you want several.

JOSEPHINE-CHARLOTTE: At least two, but they've got to arrive at the same time.

MARIE-ANTOINETTE: Twins?

JOSEPHINE-CHARLOTTE: Maybe. . .but then you'd have to have three or four at a shot.

MARIE-ANTOINETTE: I don't get it.

JOSEPHINE-CHARLOTTE: It's quite simple really. We'd have to make sure that both our babies were delivered at the same time, so they'd always be the same age. No age difference, no complications. The two of us breast feed them at the same time, take them to the nursery at the same time, teach them to speak, to walk, to swim, to ride a bike, all at the same time. One thing at a time and all in the right order. I say that that's the right principle to follow.

MARIE-ANTOINETTE: And the fathers?

JOSEPHINE-CHARLOTTE: Who knows? But you've got a point there. Two fathers would be better than one.

MARIE-ANTOINETTE: Why?

JOSEPHINE-CHARLOTTE: So everything's fair and square. Can you imagine one man taking responsibility for babies? It'd go right to his head.

MARIE-ANTOINETTE: But they'd never agree to that!

JOSEPHINE-CHARLOTTE: You really don't think so? I thought you knew men, since you hang around so many of them.

MARIE-ANTOINETTE: Dollars to donuts, they won't want to share. That's exactly my problem.

JOSEPHINE-CHARLOTTE: They wouldn't have to share anything at all. Each gets one mother, and each gets one kid. No uncle, no godfather. We're against ambiguity. I'm totally opposed to it.

MARIE-ANTOINETTE: Are you going to go around looking for sperm donors?

JOSEPHINE-CHARLOTTE: Do you imagine that we'd let ourselves be injected with the divine seed of total strangers? And risk bringing complete defectives into the world? You think that I went to the trouble of studying genetics for my health? We want to know and the kids have a right to know. And what happens if Lorraine and me both ran straight into a tree or were in an airplane crash. . . there must be a father. There's got to be some backup for these children.

MARIE-ANTOINETTE: You'll have to find a way to seduce these hypothetical Dads. Everything will need to be synchronized down to the minute.

JOSEPHINE-CHARLOTTE: I don't need to tell you how fast it takes for a man to get interested. Especially when he thinks *you're* only interested in one thing. It's all the other stuff that holds them back: feelings, moral sermons, solemn promises, and so on and so on. At the end of an evening after a lot of boozing, we become, in a certain sense, like the cherries on the cake.

MARIE-ANTOINETTE: And Lorraine thinks this is normal? For you to cheat on her. . . with a man? Do you?

JOSEPHINE-CHARLOTTE: Of course. If it was with another woman, it would be a mortal blow. But doing it this way, what difference does it make? And anyway, having a man from time to time might be fun.

MARIE-ANTOINETTE: I wish you the best of luck. . . but forgive me if I maintain a healthy skepticism.

JOSEPHINE-CHARLOTTE: There are slews of single men out there nursing their wounds from being rejected. That's not who we're looking for. We require serious minded men with strong principles: fathers of serious-minded families.

MARIE-ANTOINETTE: To each her problems! I have no idea how to help you out. You want to populate the earth. Me, if it keeps going along this way, I'll be under the ground pretty soon. If one of them tries to introduce me to the other, what do I do then?

JOSEPHINE-CHARLOTTE: You're not going to let this be the end of the line; you have plenty of cards up your sleeve. You've been through a million like this already. Trust your instinct.

MARIE-ANTOINETTE: Well no, at this point, I'm pretty much up the creek without a paddle. I anticipated everything, everything except this. You do realize that when we're lying in bed, they're talking about me, and then about the other. . . the other me, I mean. Oh, I just don't see any way out of this.

JOSEPHINE-CHARLOTTE: There is no way out.

MARIE-ANTOINETTE: What did you say?

JOSEPHINE-CHARLOTTE: Can't you see where you stand? You're saturated. Put a lid on it. Just let it drop.

MARIE-ANTOINETTE: It's not as easy as you think, Josephine-Charlotte. I'm attached to these two men, me, to these two yummy guys. They're adorable and they adore me too. I'm their whole world. I can feel it. If you only knew what they say to each other about me! It's enough to make you weep.

JOSEPHINE-CHARLOTTE: Not in my shop, please!

MARIE-ANTOINETTE: I need both, don't you understand? What should I do if push comes to shove?

JOSEPHINE-CHARLOTTE: Just stall. The longer the better.

MARIE-ANTOINETTE: I already said I had a seminar I had to attend.

JOSEPHINE-CHARLOTTE: That's one obvious solution. You could also enter a convent and wait till it all blows over.

MARIE-ANTOINETTE: If only I could stand living without them.

JOSEPHINE-CHARLOTTE: Listen, who knows? Tomorrow, one might develop an allergy to chlorine, or the other might change his mind about planting a garden the size of a postage stamp. What's the rush? Come on, give us a smile! . . . And in the meantime, what say we have a little pick-me-up!

## SCENE TEN

*One evening, in* JULIAN*'s apartment.*

JULIAN: How did your seminar go?

ANTOINETTE: Oh, the boss was all hyped on himself, as usual. And this time, he had company. It was a duo, him and a big mucky-muck from the agency, some conceited asshole! Who do they think they are anyway? One day they dream up a slogan for laundry detergent and call themselves "creative entities." All it means is that they're liable to go on for two hours at a stretch about whether the girl on the poster should be blonde or brunette, or if the boy should be clean-shaven or have two days' worth of stubble.

JULIAN: I guess they have to justify their fees somehow!

ANTOINETTE: You should give it a whirl. I bet your slogans would wipe them all off the charts.

JULIAN: I don't see why.

ANTOINETTE: You know all there is to know about words, don't you?

JULIAN: Yes, I pick them out, I appreciate them. . . but it's a long way from there to the world you're talking about! I have a hard time seeing myself giving deep thought to dishwashing detergents and pampers day in and day out.

ANTOINETTE: So you'd prefer putting the pampers on yourself?

JULIAN: Me, pampers?

ANTOINETTE: Not on you, on babies! I mean . . . babies you'd have to change.

JULIAN: Oh, well, that never entered my mind. . . I'd need to give it some thought. . . Why did you say that? Are you pregnant?

ANTOINETTE: Are you kidding! I was only trying to figure you out, that's all. So kids wouldn't be your cup of tea?

JULIAN: I wouldn't say that. I'm not opposed to the idea in principle. You're the one who'd have to want it, naturally, but I guess I could see myself. . . not changing his diaper maybe. . . but it'd be fun. I could teach him things.

ANTOINETTE: Clearly you expect it to be a boy.

JULIAN: Why do you say that?

ANTOINETTE: Because you said change *his* diaper, not *her* diaper.

JULIAN: Sorry, but that's the way it is! But I repeat, you're the one who'd have to. . .

ANTOINETTE: Why not us?

JULIAN: Or us, if you say so.

ANTOINETTE: So, me then, if I want it so much. But why wouldn't you be the one who makes the final decision?

JULIAN: Because. . . because that's not how it works. It's your body. I couldn't be a mere stand-in. . . I just wouldn't choose that for myself.

ANTOINETTE: You think your plate's full enough as it is. Why pile on yet another responsibility?!

JULIAN: What I was trying to say. . .

ANTOINETTE: Being a modern man's a cushy deal it seems.

JULIAN: I never said I was a modern man. I'd say I'd identify more as conservative. But what's been achieved's been achieved, and there's no turning back.

ANTOINETTE: Never any reason to change, right?

JULIAN: It's not my fault. It's got nothing to do with me. Why don't you ask all your buddies what they think?

ANTOINETTE: What buddies? I don't have any buddies. . . please note, the word is asexual. Because basically you're my buddy.

JULIAN: Your roommate.

ANTOINETTE: Room? Alcove, more like; or mezzanine.

JULIAN: I do acknowledge that. We are a bit cramped here. It hit me when I was back at Adrian's place.

ANTOINETTE: Adrian?

JULIAN: My garden architect, the one who's going to bring the countryside into this apartment. He's got the most charming little farmhouse. You should come and see it. The bedroom looks out over a garden. . . Words can't express! You'd love it.

ANTOINETTE: So you saw his bedroom?

JULIAN: From the garden. A very pretty bedroom. Really romantic.

ANTOINETTE: It made you jealous?

JULIAN: The farmhouse? Yes, a little. But he's constantly tormenting himself whether he should move back into town. When it comes down to it, no one's ever really happy.

ANTOINETTE: Did you see his girlfriend?

JULIAN: No, unfortunately. He says he's sorry he hasn't met you yet either. He says hi anyway.

ANTOINETTE: But I've never even seen this guy.

JULIAN: It's a vicarious friendship. Same on my end. Ever since he mentioned this Marie I have a real strong urge to meet her.

ANTOINETTE: So she interests you?

JULIAN: There's no need to be jealous.

ANTOINETTE: I'm not jealous. How could I be jealous?

JULIAN: You're right. But the friends of our friends are our friends, so naturally this Adrian. . .

ANTOINETTE: So since this Adrian seems to have become your friend, it means he's my friend too, is that it?

JULIAN: But no hanky-panky, of course.

ANTOINETTE: No hanky-panky, just as you say.

JULIAN: Why? You think it's a throwback to insist on that? Does that make me a nerd?

ANTOINETTE: Oh Julian, what exactly are you cooking up?

JULIAN: Just that we want to arrange a little something. . .

ANTOINETTE: Who is this "we?"

JULIAN: Adrian and me.

ANTOINETTE: Oh boy, somebody's got a crush!

JULIAN: We can't go on shut away like this. We never go out together. . . This'd be the perfect opportunity. We picked out a restaurant. The Vaudeville, it's called. An old theatre. How about it?

ANTOINETTE: I bet it was you who picked out the restaurant.

JULIAN: I can't hide anything from you.

ANTOINETTE: But Marie would have to want to go too!

JULIAN: I love the way you say that, as if you've known each other all your lives.

ANTOINETTE: I hope it's mutual.

JULIAN: Of course. If the two of you didn't get along it'd be a real shame.

ANTOINETTE: Anything's possible. But just because you guys get along doesn't mean we have to.

JULIAN: That would surprise me. You have so many things in common. I understand that she turns up at his place without any warning, same as you. Fortunately when you get your cell phone. . .

ANTOINETTE: I changed my mind. It was a dumb idea. I was tempted for one tiny little second. At first I thought it'd make me feel freer, but in fact, you just become a slave to this thing. You were right all along.

JULIAN: What a shame!

ANTOINETTE: I didn't get the feeling you really wanted me to.

JULIAN: Well, it would have helped me to reach you anytime I wanted, any hour of the day or night.

ANTOINETTE: That's exactly what made me reconsider.

JULIAN: So are we on for the restaurant?

ANTOINETTE: Leave me a message at the office. I'll call you this afternoon. It depends on one or two things.

JULIAN: He'll be so pleased!

## SCENE ELEVEN

*End of the afternoon, in* ADRIAN*'s house.*

MARIE: The sunsets here are more beautiful.

ADRIAN: More beautiful than where?

MARIE: Than anywhere else, I'm sure of it.

ADRIAN: It's true. You must have plenty of places to compare it to since you're so well travelled.

MARIE: It must be a question of roots... You were right about the magnolia. You really ought to plant it in your garden.

ADRIAN: What magnolia?

MARIE: My grandmother's.

ADRIAN: I thought you meant Julian's. Absurd, of course... Strange you talking about roots. It's not like you.

MARIE: What exactly are the roots of people?

ADRIAN: I've no idea. Ancestors, parents. . .

MARIE: Children too maybe. They sprout up from below like roots.

ADRIAN: What's wrong Marie? I've never seen you looking so serious.

MARIE: I really could imagine children scampering around this garden.

ADRIAN: Me too. Sometimes I think about it. And then I forget it.

MARIE: It's not up to you to decide, right?

ADRIAN: No, it's for two people. . .

MARIE: I'm here.

ADRIAN: I know.

MARIE: So, you couldn't see me in that role?

ADRIAN: Let's just say, not yet. I think I'd feel something if. . . it's the kind of thing you'd feel.

MARIE: And can you see yourself in that kind of role?

ADRIAN: I'd like to have been born a woman. Just for that reason. To produce a child and then sit staring at it. . . same as when I sit there watching my trees growing.

MARIE: Then I'm not the one you need.

ADRIAN: I repeat, there's a time for everything. I'm in no rush. I watch you growing too.

MARIE: Sometimes I think to myself I'll never put down roots here. I love moving around too much. I can't stay in one place. It'll get me from behind somewhere else.

ADRIAN: Something's going on inside that's eating at you.

MARIE: Yes, something I'm considering. They made me an offer down at the office today. Our representative in Mexico has handed in her notice.

The position's available immediately. Lots of reservations for Mexico have already come in this year, and we can't let the visitors land without having someone on the spot to give them a proper welcome. The boss thought of me before opening a wider search. I can get by pretty well in Spanish. It's an attractive proposition.

ADRIAN: Will you be gone a long time?

MARIE: Six months exactly. I'd have my own apartment there.

ADRIAN: You should accept.

MARIE: Wouldn't you miss me?

ADRIAN: What kind of question is that! But I know there's no point trying to keep you here. I'm not going to get down on my knees, or beg you to stay.

MARIE: I'd love it if someone begged me to stay.

ADRIAN: I'm not sure it would make any difference. . .

MARIE: You're right. It's pure vanity on my part.

ADRIAN: Once you're there, you'll have a chance to mull it over.

MARIE: What?

ADRIAN: What you're really looking for. And if you decide you want me to fly out and join you, you can tell me what it's worth to you.

MARIE: Well, we shall see! The profits to be had are nothing to sneeze at.

ADRIAN: I bet the sunsets in Mexico aren't too dusty either.

MARIE: You're a true friend, Adrian.

ADRIAN: I hope I can be more than that.

MARIE: There's nothing more beautiful than friendship. It can weather whatever may come along. I implore you, if I ever do go away, don't sit there crying your heart out waiting for me to come back. There must be loads of girls out there just dying to make you happy. And you do know how to make a girl happy. They can sense it, you know. They have a nose for it, same as you.

ADRIAN: Marie, you're gibbering. You're not the same anymore. Is it this choice you're facing that's got you so down?

MARIE: I've never been very good at making choices. And here I am up against a real hoop. I can't avoid it. I've just got to jump through it.

ADRIAN: We should talk it over with Julian. Nothing simpler. We're having dinner together tomorrow at the Vaudeville, and we'll invite his girlfriend.

MARIE: Antoinette?

ADRIAN: Antoinette, yes that's the one. Julian's a really interesting person. I'm positive he'll be able to give you some sound advice.

MARIE: But he doesn't even know me. What more could he say than you already have? You've sensed exactly what's happening to me, and you've said all there is to say, Adrian. You're like a brother to me.

ADRIAN: So now I'm a brother?! Why not a Jewish mother?

MARIE: Or a Mexican one?

ADRIAN: Are you coming tomorrow?

MARIE: The boss gave me twenty-four hours to mull it over. I've got to give him my answer tomorrow at noon. If it's yes, I'll leave the following evening. I'll have just enough time to pack my bags. In that case, better count me out.

ADRIAN: What about your visa?

MARIE: My visa's still valid for a few weeks. I'll get it extended once I'm there.

ADRIAN: Then you won't get to meet Julian.

MARIE: Oh. . . you can introduce me to him sometime in the future. And anyway who knows? Maybe you could bring him along with you to Mexico someday.

ADRIAN: Certainly not. If I only get to be with you for a few days, I won't be sharing you with somebody else!

MARIE: You really are the bomb, Adrian. Guys like you don't grow on trees. I'm already looking forward to when I get to see you again.

ADRIAN: We're not there yet. This evening is ours though. We've got lots of reasons for uncorking the champagne. . .

MARIE: Your garden?

ADRIAN: My park, you mean. I'm told they really went wild about the idea at the local neighborhood board. The mayor has yet to sign off on it, but that's apparently just a formality.

MARIE: My spending a few nights here paid off then.

ADRIAN: Do you know, the evening you came, I pushed it right up to the last possible minute, with barely enough time to deliver the plans before the deadline passed.

MARIE: Did you include magnolias?

ADRIAN: Loads of magnolias everywhere. And then I suggested they call it "The Avenue of Magnolias."

MARIE: And they went for it?

ADRIAN: I'd be amazed if they did.

MARIE: Then it'll be our own private name. For all time.

## SCENE TWELVE

*A table in restaurant, The Vaudeville.* JULIAN *and* ADRIAN *are sitting down to dinner.*

ADRIAN: You came by yourself?

JULIAN: So did you!

ADRIAN: I'll explain. How about you?

JULIAN: Oh, for me it's the same old same old. We never go anywhere together. In the beginning it was a little weird, but I got used to it. She always had some good reason.

ADRIAN: And you never go and pick her up?

JULIAN: You'd think!

ADRIAN: You don't mean to tell me you don't even know where she lives?

JULIAN: It's as if she lives in her office. That's where I always connect with her... when I do manage to find her. She's always on the telephone. She must live in a telephone, a gigantic telephone. Like the cabin in a spaceship: compact but comfortable.

ADRIAN: You don't seem to mind all that much.

JULIAN: It's just this way she has of being inaccessible. Women always have to be inaccessible. Somehow... Don't you find?

ADRIAN: Well, for me, women... I only really know one. At least I think I know one. And that's where it stops. And I like it like that.

JULIAN: Why? If you surrounded yourself with women wouldn't that disperse the issue?

ADRIAN: No, I find one woman is already a whole world to herself...or a garden if you like.

JULIAN: Now you're a poet!

ADRIAN: No, just a professional. I can only compare her to what I already know. A garden has it all: something hard, something tender, beautiful, something cruel even, and it's changing all the time, even if it's almost imperceptible. You'll see when you have your own. You'll never be able to leave it once you've gotten genuinely attached to it.

JULIAN: I wouldn't take the risk of separating from it. It's something I've wanted so much. Never thought I'd ever have one. An oasis in the desert... How about your dreams of a life in the city?

ADRIAN: All it takes is for me to drive her in for me to lose my interest in it. It took me ages to find a place to park.

JULIAN: You should have put it in the parking lot, just a few steps down the block.

ADRIAN: I hate parking lots. Especially underground garages. I literally start to choke when I'm underground, and after I can never find where I put the damn thing. I run around in circles, start to panic. Break into a sweat. I could tell you some real horror stories. Never again!

JULIAN: But as an architect, you must have a good sense of direction.

ADRIAN: When you're in a maze there's no fixed point. Everything starts to look the same. They're designed deliberately to disorient you. You lose due North, and you don't even have the sky as a reference. I'm sure that compasses wouldn't even work down there.

JULIAN: Oh. . . so you study the stars?

ADRIAN: At night, all the time. I love it. When the sky is clear it chills me right out. When I'm buried in work and I feel all locked-up inside, or feel like I'm about to doze off on my papers, I just stare out at the sky. Makes me feel like I'm somehow communing with the universe.

JULIAN: I'd like you to show me some time. . . How about Marie?

ADRIAN: She's got a problem. Well, it's me, actually. But she seems to be handling it pretty well.

JULIAN: She's seeing a doctor?

ADRIAN: A doctor? No, you've got it wrong. . . She might actually relocate abroad. And if things fall into place, tomorrow or the next day she'll be heading off, far away.

JULIAN: Where to?

ADRIAN: Mexico.

JULIAN: That's not the ends of the world.

ADRIAN: There are no more ends of the world, that's true. . . but this is hard for me to take. I'm not sure what to make of it.

JULIAN: She's off on a trip?

ADRIAN: No, it's for her job. Six months at least.

JULIAN: Why, at least?

ADRIAN: Because I know she'll love it over there. Mexico's just her kind of place. If she doesn't show up here tonight, that means she's going through with it, no doubt about it.

JULIAN: She's got to see somebody, sign a contract?

ADRIAN: Yes, and if she is taking off, she'll have to pack her bags this very evening.

JULIAN: If she's anything like Antoinette, that'll be a big deal. I sometimes think she has two of everything.

ADRIAN: I've never seen her closet, but Marie isn't too dusty in that department either.

JULIAN: You've never seen her closet? Tell you the truth, neither have I, but I just somehow imagined it.

ADRIAN: Strange, though. . . women these days keep so many funny secrets.

JULIAN: Well they need to compensate, don't they. Time was when they couldn't even bare their ankles. Now it's their closets. Must be a connection.

ADRIAN: You don't look too upset about Antoinette.

JULIAN: True, but one thing I don't like. I really wanted the two of you to meet. She was supposed to have called me this afternoon, but she didn't, so I guess something came up.

ADRIAN: So end of story? Don't you want to find out what's what?

JULIAN: I prefer it this way. I couldn't stand it if she started asking endless questions about my life either.

ADRIAN: Because she'd have something to ask about?

JULIAN: From a certain point of view. . . doubtless a somewhat archaic point of view—archaeological.

ADRIAN: I don't see the connection with archaeology.

JULIAN: You forget that I've gone into the subject in depth. I'm an archaeologist digging into human morals. Barely a century ago—and a century's nothing on a scale with the solar system. Barely a century ago everything was absolutely socially cubby-holed and regulated. You were a prisoner, a total victim of societal or conjugal surveillance. It was a hellish existence. Today we can see the humor in it. . . but only when we see it on stage, and theatre isn't real life! You can't imagine how much weeping and gnashing of teeth it all caused. So give me anything but that, and Antoinette is pretty much on the same page as me.

ADRIAN: So you do whatever you feel like?

JULIAN: We could do what we feel like, but that's a very good reason not to, since there's no line to cross. There's no transgression to commit. If you take away the barrier, you take away the pleasure in violating it.

ADRIAN: So no more desire.

JULIAN: No more desire. . . or practically none.

ADRIAN: So what have you been staring at all this time? Seems like your eyes are. . .

JULIAN: You're on to something. You'll know soon enough, but easy does it. Whatever you do, don't turn around. Besides, I do believe there's a mirror behind me. Haven't you noticed anything special?

ADRIAN: Not really. I just see some fairly ordinary couples. The guys, I can only see their backs, the women, nothing much to speak of. . . Oh yes, now I see what you mean: A gorgeous ficus, in splendid condition, clearly. It's most surprising that a ficus should flourish in a place like this.

JULIAN: That's not the only thing that's flourishing here, believe me. Wait, I'll just edge forwards a couple of inches, discreetly. So now you can have a clear view.

ADRIAN: Are you talking about those two girls?

JULIAN: Two women you mean.

ADRIAN: I said that for the benefit of the one who has her back turned to us. Short hair, exposed neck that makes her look younger. Let me just lean forward a drop. I want to see her face in the other mirror. She's gorgeous!

JULIAN: For the record, I don't think you noticed, but just a moment ago she was giving me the high sign. That's all I have to say.

ADRIAN: You mean she winked at you?

JULIAN: Don't be gross. More delicate, more discreet. Just squeezing her earlobe ever so slightly, just being off-handed. Or ever so gently lifting her foot out of her shoe. Oh, women!

ADRIAN: What about women?

JULIAN: Just to say they don't have much wiggle room. We see a chick we like, we saunter over to their table, offer them a drink, and it all goes like clockwork. But how about them?

ADRIAN: I thought times had changed, that it was all archaeology and so forth.

JULIAN: No, I think there's still a ways to go. Besides, I'm not really sure it would represent progress anyway. If we didn't have this game to play a certain charm would be lost. You have to understand them, that's all. I'm genuinely moved when a woman dares to cross the line of what's permitted with the modest means at her disposal. Obviously it's far easier in an elevator, a bus, or a train, where promiscuity has immediate impact, where a guy could even be forced into it. But if she sees someone who really turns her on in a social hub like a restaurant, what are the chances? She can only pray that the guy has antennae.

ADRIAN: So you think she's got the hots for you?

JULIAN: You'll be able to verify that in just a moment.

ADRIAN: Really? But what if Antoinette showed up?

JULIAN: She's not coming now, I told you. And as for Marie, you can forget her too. You'd better change your way of looking at it, or else you'll find yourself sinking into a depression.

ADRIAN: I don't have the right attitude for all this.

JULIAN: You just said she was cute.

ADRIAN: That's no reason to force myself on her.

JULIAN: You really think you'd be forcing yourself on them? Why do you think they go out together? Because they wouldn't dare to on their own. So they close ranks. And then they tell each other they've made out like bandits.

ADRIAN: Don't you think they might have boyfriends, being so pretty and all that?

JULIAN: What difference would that make? Here they are, totally available, served up like those pheasants they just got served. Pheasants are tasty, so that proves they have good taste. They took a table for four, which also tells us something. I say we walk right over there. But before we do, one sound piece of advice. Basic caution dictates that we not divulge our real identity. Your name is Hadrian, and you're a gym teacher, and I'm Dorian, a history teacher. And we both teach at Grimm Brothers High School.

## SCENE THIRTEEN

MARIE-ANTOINETTE *and* JOSEPHINE-CHARLOTTE *are on the telephone.*

JOSEPHINE-CHARLOTTE: What, to Mexico? That's great, sweetie!

MARIE-ANTOINETTE: It's quite a plunge to take. I'm leaving tomorrow. I've already locked my suitcases. But, still. . . I don't know if I'm doing the right thing.

JOSEPHINE-CHARLOTTE: You have to follow your intuition. You've got good instincts. I'm sure you know what you're doing, even if in another way you're totally clueless.

MARIE-ANTOINETTE: I guess, but it's hard. It's all happening so fast. . . That girl who resigned, the way it fell right in my lap. . . Last night while I was packing my bags I had to stop several times to cry. It just hit me like a ton of bricks, you have no idea.

JOSEPHINE-CHARLOTTE: It's obvious that it was dawning on you that what you're doing is an important step in your life. Sure, it must feel like a game of emotional pinball, but I have no doubt that you're on the right track.

MARIE-ANTOINETTE: You're sure?

JOSEPHINE-CHARLOTTE: Yes, and I'm rarely mistaken. This is just the sort of thing you need. A clean break. This double life you're leading can't go on indefinitely.

MARIE-ANTOINETTE: Double life? No it wasn't. It was my life pure and simple. I really felt like I was completely there inside of it.

JOSEPHINE-CHARLOTTE: There, you see? You're already speaking about it in the past tense.

MARIE-ANTOINETTE: I suppose, but I just can't wrap my mind around it. I was so happy, you have no idea.

JOSEPHINE-CHARLOTTE: It wouldn't have worked in the long run. The moment would inevitably come when you'd be cornered.

MARIE-ANTOINETTE: Maybe it would have all have worked out. They were on the right track. They were getting to know each other. They were discovering all these things they had in common. . .

JOSEPHINE-CHARLOTTE: Yeah, so long as one of the main things they had in common never showed her face.

MARIE-ANTOINETTE: What?

JOSEPHINE-CHARLOTTE: You of course! Do I need to draw a map for you?

MARIE-ANTOINETTE: Are you so sure? Some arrangements of that sort have been known to work.

JOSEPHINE-CHARLOTTE: That's all they ever are—arrangements. Two women and a man. . . On a wing and a prayer it could be made to work. But two men and a woman, that's a whole other ball of wax. First you'd have to be sure that the first relationship was rock solid, and then gradually get the third party used to the idea. With you, it's the total opposite. Can't you see the risk you'd be running? They're both gonna come crashing down, I'm warning you. And don't expect the more open-minded one to accept this revolutionary situation you're dragging him into either. Their male pride would be wounded, and they'd only have one of two options—drop you entirely or resign themselves to it. And you can't bear resigned people, if I recall correctly.

MARIE-ANTOINETTE: You're right as usual Charlotte. But I feel like I'm jumping ship.

JOSEPHINE-CHARLOTTE: Not at all. It's just that life has come to your rescue. Life can be like that. You can count on life to be there for you now and then, but then you'd better recognize a chance when it's being offered. And you can always count on us too, Lorraine and me. Mexico connects both of us. We'll come and visit you. I've decided to hire an assistant so I can take more time off. I've had it with being glued to this counter twenty-four hours a day. And Lorraine'll work it out as well. You'll be seeing a lot more of us than you think. And anyway, six months isn't the rest of your life. The whole thing might resolve itself by then.

MARIE-ANTOINETTE: What thing?

JOSEPHINE-CHARLOTTE: One of the two'll get tired of waiting. It's the best test, all things considered. It won't be long before they console themselves. Men know how to dust themselves off pretty well, in general. . . Oh, and by the way, I wanted you to know, Lorraine and I have gone and done it!

MARIE-ANTOINETTE: Done what?

JOSEPHINE-CHARLOTTE: We actually threw down, just like two ordinary straight women. It wasn't exactly like seeing the star of Bethlehem, but it was a lot less unpleasant than a normal trip to the G.Y.N.

MARIE-ANTOINETTE: Oh, I'm so happy for you both! You didn't waste any time, did you?

JOSEPHINE-CHARLOTTE: Have you ever known me to procrastinate once I get an idea in my head?

MARIE-ANTOINETTE: And were they nice?

JOSEPHINE-CHARLOTTE: Couldn't have been nicer! Stumbling on two recruits like that the first night of draft call! And followed all the proper etiquette to boot, foraging through their wallets. Started off pretty hesitant, then turned into eager beavers when we said we weren't interested in using condoms. And when they heard I was a pharmacist, they became totally trusting. This job has certain advantages after all. It's a seal of approval! If they only knew! In my line of work it seems, the shoemaker's always the one wearing the worst shoes. But anyway, it's all for a good cause. Now, we'll just have to wait and see.

MARIE-ANTOINETTE: What are you talking about! Aren't you ashamed of yourselves, treating them like that?

JOSEPHINE-CHARLOTTE: Hanh! I'm supposed to be upset now that the shoe's on the other foot?! Anyway, who says we won't be seeing them again? That'll be just one more test. The way they came onto us—especially one of the two—it was obviously not his first time. I spotted him in a jiffy. A good-looking guy, slick talker, totally sure of himself. The second I gave him a look, he picked up on it. Quick on the uptake. Made his move. He obviously didn't want to leave his pal high and dry. It was clear he'd had to talk him into being part of it, but in no time the whole thing started taking off great guns. And since Lorraine had been staring at his buddy, that greased the wheels. He wasn't in as big a rush as mine was, and harder to loosen up, but Lorraine, she's so sentimental, she kind of liked him for being like that. But the ends justified the means. We weren't going to waste every night of the week cruising in restaurants; we had to get on with our lives you know. It was right in the middle of our Rock Cornish hens that they struck. No sooner had we finished our appetizers than they walked over and parked themselves across from us. I didn't waste any time harpooning them, and after that it was child's play. I'd forgotten how easy it is to pick up a guy. You won't have any trouble finding one over in Mexico; I hear they get turned on at the drop of a hat. But they're not going to be very open to sharing you I'm told. Oh no, they're too macho for that.

MARIE-ANTOINETTE: So what were your two sperm donors like?

JOSEPHINE-CHARLOTTE: Damn good, the two of them. One more of a jock than the other—he was a gym teacher and lived out in the country. And as Lorraine managed to glean later, his wife had just left him or something. But Lorraine knows how to give consolation to souls in torment. She simply explained to him—she's not a psychologist for nothing—that it was just a stage in mourning for the lost relationship, and that this was the best strategy for managing the pain. The other one, mine, well I didn't get any sense that I was dealing with a grief stricken soul. . . Marie-Antoinette? . . . Are you there? Did we get cut off? Can you hear me?

MARIE-ANTOINETTE: What was the name of this restaurant you were in?

JOSEPHINE-CHARLOTTE: It was some renovated theatre. Let's see if I can remember. . . The Vaudeville, yes that's it, the Vaudeville. . . Why are you coughing like that?

## SCENE FOURTEEN

*One morning, in* JULIAN*'s apartment.*

ANTOINETTE: I came to tell you that I'm off.

JULIAN: You too?

ANTOINETTE: Why me too?

JULIAN: You know that architect I had dinner with last night? His girlfriend's leaving too. To Mexico! Would you believe it?

ANTOINETTE: What's there to believe? Will she be gone long?

JULIAN: Six months, at least six months.

ANTOINETTE: Oh well, I'm leaving too.

JULIAN: You're kidding! For how long?

ANTOINETTE: Six months. That's a good length of time. Six months.

JULIAN: And where are you going?

ANTOINETTE: Nowhere. But you'll never see me again. I'm dropping out of your life, that's all.

JULIAN: Do you have a good reason?

ANTOINETTE: More like a feeling. I've got to go. And anyway why should I give you reasons? You never asked for any before, so why now?

JULIAN: Let's just say I never said anything. It never entered my mind to. I'm sorry.

ANTOINETTE: It just hit me yesterday afternoon. I asked myself why I was calling you when I had no real desire to see you.

JULIAN: There's a first time for everything. We've never seen a soul, both of us together. We left our cocoon for the first time. It must have disoriented you.

ANTOINETTE: Not exactly, but you're not that far off. I just can't see myself by your side with other people there. I can't see myself associating with you in public, if you like. That must be telling us something surely? So, I thought it'd just be better to let time take its course. Does what I'm saying have legs?

JULIAN: Yes. You don't want for social acceptance, the gaze of others, to determine how you act. . . That certainly makes sense. Maybe we've been living in too confined a space, too closed in on ourselves. And that when I invited you to this dinner, everything must have seemed out of kilter to you. I sensed right away that you weren't exactly thrilled at the prospect. But from that point to this decision you've made. . .

ANTOINETTE: What do you really think about it, deep down, in your soul?

JULIAN: In the first place, it's not for me to go against anything you wanted. If that's the way you feel, why would I ever call it into question?

ANTOINETTE: But doesn't that just leave a void?

JULIAN: In my life you mean? Of course! It hasn't hit me yet, it's all so new. I'll see how I feel tonight or tomorrow. I'll call you at the office.

ANTOINETTE: No way. I don't want you calling me anymore. There'd be no reason to.

JULIAN: Whatever you want.

ANTOINETTE: So, did you have a good time last night?

JULIAN: Yes. . .well, no. Marie didn't show up either. Adrian was crushed. She was packing her suitcases.

ANTOINETTE: And you consoled each other?

JULIAN: What do you mean? You mean, did I console him?

ANTOINETTE: Yes, that's right.

JULIAN: Oh, you know how it is with guys.

ANTOINETTE: Actually I don't. I don't know how it is.

JULIAN: You try to make the best of it. You kid around, you drink.

ANTOINETTE: Did you have a lot to drink?

JULIAN: A fair amount, yes.

ANTOINETTE: You don't look it.

JULIAN: I can hold my liquor, as you know. But Adrian. . . you should have seen him. He was under the table.

ANTOINETTE: You gave me the impression that he really cared for this Marie.

JULIAN: Obviously. Before the night was through he was calling everyone Marie.

ANTOINETTE: Who is everyone?

JULIAN: I don't know, the cigarette storeowner, the lady in the cloakroom.

ANTOINETTE: Because he was buying cigarettes? That's not his thing.

JULIAN: How do you know that?

ANTOINETTE: The way you described him to me, man of the woods and all. I saw him more with a meerschaum pipe, watching his goats frolicking in the pasture.

JULIAN: Boy you're intuitive! That's him to a tee.

ANTOINETTE: So aside from the cigarette storeowner and the cloakroom attendant there weren't other women around?

JULIAN: Sure, it was packed. But it was all couples. This restaurant is the kind you go to as a couple or with friends, not to meet new people.

ANTOINETTE: Except the cloakroom lady and the cigarette seller, if she's well-stacked, of course.

JULIAN: You're being pretty sarcastic today.

ANTOINETTE: Call it what you will. It's just my way of making sure that you won't miss me.

JULIAN: Of course I'll miss you, if that's what you're worried about. But it's not cool to make yourself seem worse than you are.

ANTOINETTE: Why, because it makes a mark on the pretty picture? I suppose you'd rather be in the slough of despond, just so you can complain about it afterwards?

JULIAN: I'd never complain on account of that. If you want to put all this time and distance between us, then that's what I deserve. I have only myself to blame. I love you, anyone can see that. Maybe my way of showing it is less easy to see. I haven't had time to make sense of it, since you're taking off so suddenly. I'm not going start clinging to you, because that might make you change your mind for all the wrong reasons. But it's clear that tomorrow, or next week, or whenever I least expect it, I'll get a lump in my throat, and I won't know why, because I'll be overcome by fear. Fear that I'll never hold you in my arms again. You matter to me, Antoinette. I can't exactly articulate precisely to what extent; but you do matter, and you always will.

ANTOINETTE: It's kind of you to say that Julian.

JULIAN: By the way, what are you doing with the magnolia?

ANTOINETTE: What do you think?

JULIAN: I only mention the magnolia because... There's nothing else to mention. Since that's the only thing I've got of you here.

ANTOINETTE: It seems to be doing fine.

JULIAN: I've never put so much energy into a plant in my life, thanks in large part to Adrian's excellent advice.

ANTOINETTE: Then keep it.

JULIAN: Thank you. For everything.

## SCENE FIFTEEN

*Early afternoon, in* ADRIAN*'s house.*

MARIE: I came to tell you I'm leaving.

ADRIAN: I suspected as much. You didn't show up last night, so I put two and two together pretty quick. I knew that if you'd been able to come, you'd have been exactly on time, same as ever. Wound up being just the two of us.

MARIE: Antoinette didn't turn up either?

ADRIAN: We just sat there like a couple of jerks, our noses in our plates.

MARIE: Well she must have had a good reason, just like me.

ADRIAN: Julian said she never gives a reason. And that he never asked for one.

MARIE: A thoroughly modern couple, those two.

ADRIAN: Like you say. That's so pathetic.

MARIE: You spent the evening pretty down and dirty, if I'm not mistaken.

ADRIAN: Not really. From a certain angle.

MARIE: Which angle is that?

ADRIAN: Well, to tell you the truth, it wasn't just the two of us for all that long.

MARIE: There was someone there you were cruising?

ADRIAN: Call it what you will.

MARIE: You, on the prowl in a fashionable restaurant, I'd have loved to have seen that.

ADRIAN: You think I'm incapable of such a thing? You seem to find it funny?

MARIE: In some sense, it reassures me.

ADRIAN: You're funny. You really are!

MARIE: Would you rather I started blubbering?

ADRIAN: No. No, I'd really rather not. It's just that you don't seem the least bit upset. It's surprising.

MARIE: Why tell me about it at all then if you thought it would cause me pain?

ADRIAN: You deserve to have a jot of pain. I'm not the only one.

MARIE: So that's why you did it? It was deliberate? You said to yourself, Marie's leaving me, so now I'm going to show her how easy it is for me to get over her, was that it?

ADRIAN: Yes and no.

MARIE: Or maybe it was Julian that dragged you into it? That's what comes of keeping bad company.

ADRIAN: No, no, not at all. Julian has nothing to do with it.

MARIE: You picked out some chick and you said to yourself: that one I'm going to have, just to show Marie what for, since she's riding off into the sunset.

ADRIAN: Something like that, if you want to put it that way.

MARIE: And Julian just sat there, watching you doing it?

ADRIAN: No, absolutely not. He had something to keep himself busy too.

MARIE: So you had a foursome?

ADRIAN: No, of course not!

MARIE: So what was she like? Now I really need to know all.

ADRIAN: Charming, gentle, very understanding, and how can I put it? A little unsure of herself at the start.

MARIE: You had to prime the pump, you mean?

ADRIAN: Yes. Well, no. Let's just say that once she saw that I wasn't embarrassed, she came around too.

MARIE: She knew just how to work you, I see.

ADRIAN: That's not the impression I had. She acted kind of strange. She was sort of clumsy. Not at all the type who goes around picking up guys.

MARIE: Well-composed?

ADRIAN: I could swear to you that it seemed totally spontaneous.

MARIE: Young, a teenager?

ADRIAN: No, no, far from it. I mean not a minor, not at all a minor.

MARIE: Was she by herself?

ADRIAN: No, with a friend.

MARIE: That Julian fucked.

ADRIAN: I don't know who fucked who. I think it was the friend who started it all. So Julian jumped on board. And that's what sparked the whole thing.

MARIE: And you, you were just lending a hand. You had to hold up your end. Anyway, thanks for telling me.

ADRIAN: I couldn't help it. I couldn't just let you go away with a lie hanging between us.

MARIE: Are you going to see each other again?

ADRIAN: Who?

MARIE: The not a minor and you.

ADRIAN: I have no idea. It's up to her. I don't know the first thing about her.

MARIE: And she about you?

ADRIAN: Julian suggested that I give a false name. But. . .

MARIE: But what?

ADRIAN: She asked me for my phone number.

MARIE: Just in case?

ADRIAN: She said to me: in six months, in a year, or sometime in between. The fact that she said six months made it easier for me.

MARIE: Why?

ADRIAN: I thought that in six months, I'd know where things stood with you.

MARIE: And in the event that the news was bad, you could go back?

ADRIAN: I didn't think it through like that. She just asked me the question, and I replied. That's all.

MARIE: Did she ask you that before or after?

ADRIAN: When we were leaving, this morning.

MARIE: Two goodbyes in one day. Poor Adrian, I'm so sorry I've screwed up your life like this.

ADRIAN: Without yours, I wouldn't have had the other.

MARIE: I know, I know. I'm touched that you spilled all the beans, in spite of everything. Really, even though you needed to get at me along the way. That too is love. Trying to mollify me wouldn't have gotten us anywhere. I hurt you. You hurt me. So now it's kind of a blood pact. Will you come and visit me?

ADRIAN: If you ask me to.

MARIE: I'd love you to, really. And anyway, they must have some magnificent gardens in Mexico.

## SCENE SIXTEEN

MARIE-ANTOINETTE *is writing a letter.*

MARIE-ANTOINETTE: Dear Josephine,

You have no idea how happy your letter made me. And I'm sure Adrian will feel the same when I let him know. Since he got here six months ago, and hasn't been able to tear himself away since. He closed down his life there long distance, sold his house, and settled in here. He managed to learn Spanish in just a few weeks. He's started to make quite a name for himself in the city. His style of garden design has a big appeal here, and since he's fascinated by the local styles, he's achieved a beautiful synthesis that pleases everyone. As for me, I've been given a permanent appointment; the boss is delighted that the envoys to Mexico don't get treated like *piñatas* anymore. I understand you not coming to visit all this time, especially after all the disappointments you've had and having your hopes dashed and everything. But at least one of you had her dreams fulfilled, though I could have told you that your plan to kill two birds with one stone was a bit unrealistic. It's not always a good idea to be trying to get two for the price of one, as you know. The very beginning was something of a monastic cure for me here. I had to pull myself together, rediscover my true identity; all the craziness had left me a little breathless. Since Adrian got here, I've had the feeling that I've been getting my sea legs back. He's so nice and he's really flourished in this climate. I felt for sure as I was taking off, that things would clarify for me. I didn't force him. Not by writing, calling, or rushing back to see him. He decided all on his own. He told me he couldn't help himself. I knew deep down I was waiting for him, and everything became clear the minute I saw him there with his knapsack getting off the plane. You say that you'd like to come visit me, or rather—us. You're more than welcome, both of you, or all three of you. I was so touched to hear that you'd named the baby Marie-Antoinette. There's no way you could know just how right that particular choice of first name is. You'll understand better, especially Lorraine, when you get here. Anyway, I'm thrilled about the epiphany that's in store. And not only for the two of you either. That's all I'll say for now. I hope these few words will encourage you to make the journey, since I can hardly wait to see all three of you. My dear Josephine-Charlotte, with all my love, a big hug to Lorraine from me, and send kisses to little Marie-Antoinette too.

Marie-Antoinette.

P.S. - Do you ever see that history teacher you met at the Vaudeville?

**CURTAIN**

## PLAYWRIGHTS

**Jacques De Decker**, an accomplished man of letters and major commentator on a wide range of cultural matters, has written numerous plays: *Jeu D'Intérieur*, *Petit Matin*, *Tranches de Dimanche*, *Fitness*, *Fenêtre sur Couple*, *Épiphanies*, which have been shown at such venues in Brussels as the Palais des Beaux-Arts, the Théâtre de l'Esprit Frappeur, Théâtre Molière, Théâtre Royal du Parc, and Théâtre Poème. He has been even more active as translator and adaptor, undertaking many plays from the British, German, and Dutch repertoires. Outside the theatre he has published several novels, including *La Grande Roue*, *Parades Amoureuses*, and *Le Ventre de la Baleine*. He has written book-length essays, as well as hundreds of theatre and book reviews as theatre critic and cultural editor-in-chief for *Le Soir* and in the revue *Marginales*, of which he is editor.

**Serge Goriely** is the author of numerous plays which shed light on the difficulty of living together, the burden of lies, and political issues, including *Realdemokracy*, *Cave Canem*, and *Kimberley*. He is also a filmmaker who has worked for Luxembourg, French, and Mexican television, directing numerous documentaries, such as *Le Grand Raid: Le Cap-terre de Feu*. His most recent films are *L'Ultimatum* and *L'Escale* which have shown at numerous international festivals. He teaches at the Université Catholique de Louvain, where he specializes in performing arts, with an emphasis on a comparative approach between theatre and cinema.

**Jean-Marie Piemme** was dramaturg for the Ensemble Théâtral Mobile, and then for Théâtre Varia in Brussels with Philippe Sireuil, where he also started as dramaturg, but rapidly became the house playwright. From 1983 to 1991 he served as Gérard Mortier's dramaturg at the Opéra National de Belgique. He wrote his first play *Neige en décembre* in 1986, which was staged the following year. Between then and now he has authored upwards of forty plays, including *Toréadors*, *Scandaleuses*, *Les Nageurs*, and *Sans Mentir*, many of which have been performed in Belgium and internationally, including various European nations, Quebec, Haiti, and the Democratic Republic of Congo. Several of his scenarios have been presented on Belgian and French television. He has also received a number of awards for his work. Website: jeanmariepiemme.be

**Pascal Vrebos** is a prolific dramatic author. Among his major works which have been staged in Belgium are *Cyclochoc* and *Le Jeu du Grand Hornu* (Théâtre National), *Entre-Chats* (Rideau de Bruxelles), *L'Imbécile* (Théâtre du Parc), *La Piaule* (Nouveau Théâtre de Belgique), *Crime magistral* and *Le Monstre que je suis* (Théâtre des Martyrs), *Lady Camilla* (Théâtre des Galéries). Several of his plays have been seen in France, such as *L'Avare II* (Festival d'Avignon), *Le Nain de Patmos* and *Les Imposteurs* (Théâtre de la Valette). Several of his other plays have been translated to English and been presented all over the United States. He gives courses at the Université Libre de la Bruxelles and elsewhere, is editor-in-chief of the magazine *Marianne Belgique*, and has his own talk show on Belgian television.

**TRANSLATOR**

**David Willinger** is the author/translator of seven other anthologies of Belgian drama; his *Maeterlinck Reader*, co-edited with Daniel Gerould, which came out in 2012, *Three Fin-de-Siècle Farces*, *Theatrical Gestures of Belgian Modernism* (all in Peter Lang's Francophone Belgian Series), as well as *Three Plays of Forbidden Love by Hugo Claus* (Susquehanna), *Ghelderode* (Host), *Four Works for the Theatre by Hugo Claus* (MESTC), and *An Anthology of Contemporary Belgian Plays, 1972-80* (Whitston). His many articles have been published in *Contemporary Theatre Review*, *Plays International*, *The Drama Review*, *Modern Drama*, *Western European Stages*, *Symposium*, etc. He is Professor of Theatre at City College and the Graduate Center, CUNY and has been awarded the Prix de Rayonnement by the Belgian government. He is currently writing a book on the Flemish director Ivo van Hove with Christel Stalpaert. He is also a playwright and director in his own right. Most recently he directed his play *The Upper Lip*, an adaptation of a novel by William Saroyan, and is preparing a production of his musical *Casterbridge* for June, 2015, both at Theater for the New City in the East Village, New York City.

**The Martin E. Segal Theatre Center (MESTC)** is a non-profit center for theatre, dance, and film affiliated with CUNY's PhD Program in Theatre. The Center's mission is to bridge the gap between academia and the professional performing arts communities both within the United States and internationally. By providing an open environment for the development of educational, community-driven, and professional projects in the performing arts, MESTC is a home to theatre scholars, students, playwrights, actors, dancers, directors, dramaturgs, and performing arts managers from the local and international theatre communities.

Through diverse programming—staged readings, theatre events, panel discussions, lectures, conferences, film screenings, dance—and a number of publications, MESTC enables artists, academics, visiting scholars, and performing arts professionals to participate actively in the advancement and appreciation of the entire range of theatrical experience. The Center presents staged readings to further the development of new and classic plays, lecture series, televised seminars featuring professional and academic luminaries, and arts in education programs, and maintains its long-standing visiting scholars-from-abroad program. In addition, the Center publishes a series of highly-regarded academic journals, as well as books, including plays in translation, written, translated, and edited by leading scholars.

www.theSegalCenter.org

**The PhD Program in Theatre, The Graduate Center, CUNY,** is one of the leading doctoral theatre programs in the United States. The Faculty includes distinguished professors, holders of endowed chairs, and internationally recognized scholars. The program trains future scholars and teachers in all the disciplines of theatre research. Faculty members edit MESTC publications, working closely with the doctoral students in theatre who perform a variety of editorial functions and learn the skills involved in the creation of books and journals.

www.web.gc.cuny.edu/theatre.org

**The MESTC Publication Wing** produces both journals and individual volumes. Journals include *Slavic and Eastern European Performance* (SEEP), *The Journal of American Drama and Theatre* (JADT), and *Western European Stages* (WES). Books include *Four Melodramas by Pixérécourt* (edited by Daniel Gerould and Marvin Carlson—both Distinguished Professors of Theatre at the CUNY Graduate Center), *Contemporary Theatre in Egypt*, *The Heirs of Molière* (edited and translated by Marvin Carlson), *Seven Plays by Stanisław Ignacy Witkiewicz* (edited and translated by Daniel Gerould), *The Arab Oedipus: Four Plays* (edited by Marvin Carlson), *Theatre Research Resources in New York City* (edited by Jessica Brater, Senior Editor Marvin Carlson), *Comedy: A Bibliography of Critical Studies in English on the Theory and Practice of Comedy in Drama, Theatre and Performance* (edited by Meghan Duffy, Senior Editor Daniel Gerould), *BAiT-Buenos Aires in Translation: Four Plays* (edited and translated by Jean Graham-Jones), *roMANIA AFTER 2000: Five New Romanian Plays* (edited by Saviana Stanescu and Daniel Gerould), *Four Plays from North Africa* (edited by Marvin Carlson), *Barcelona Plays: A Collection of New Plays by Catalan Playwrights* (edited and translated by Marion Peter Holt and Sharon G. Feldman), *Josep M. Benet i Jornet: Two Plays* (edited and translated by Marion Peter Holt), *Czech Plays: Seven New Works* (edited by Marcy Arlin, Gwynn MacDonald and Daniel Gerould), *Playwrights before the Fall* (edited by Daniel Gerould), *Timbre4* (edited and translated by Jean Graham-Jones), *Jan Fabre: The Servant of Beauty and I Am a Mistake* (edited and foreword by Frank Hentschker), *Quick Change: 28 Theatre Essays and 4 Plays in Translation* (by Daniel Gerould), *Shakespeare Made French: Four Plays by Jean-François Ducis* (edited and translated by Marvin Carlson), *New Plays from Spain: Eight Works by Seven Playwrights* (edited by Frank Hentschker), *Theatre from Medieval Cairo: The Ibn Dāniyāl Trilogy* (edited and translated by Safi Mahfouz and Marvin Carlson), *Four Plays from Syria: Sa'dallah Wannous* (edited by Safi Mahfouz and Marvin Carlson).

IN MEMORIAM: Daniel Gerould (1928–2012), MESTC Director of Publications
Martin E. Segal (1916–2012), MESTC Founder